GETTING STARTED IN
SOLO SPORTS

HELANE ZEIGER

SCHOLASTIC BOOK SERVICES
New York Toronto London Auckland Sydney Tokyo

ISBN 0-590-31590-0

12 11 10 9 8 7 6 5 4 3 2 1   3   2 3 4 5 6 7/8

Printed in the U. S. A.   01

For Ron, Mimi, Ted, and Vivian—
really good sports

CONTENTS

ACKNOWLEDGMENTS

I was overwhelmed by the support I received from so many people and organizations during the course of writing this book. Packages filled with information, tips, and photographs arrived in the mail weekly; and all the individuals I spoke to personally were so willing to provide me with what keeps a writer going — encouragement and cooperation, as well as material. Without all these contributions, I would not have been able to tell you how to get started in the solo sports and games included in this book. These are the people who made it all possible; these are the people I especially thank:

Backpacking: Gregg Mayer, Recreational Equipment, Inc.; Thomas Winnett and Penny Hargrove, Wilderness Press; Louise Marshall, American Hiking Society. **Bicycling:** Frank Wong, Square Wheel; Daniel Munch, Velo-Sport Cyclery; Raleigh Bicycle Company; Schwinn Bicycle Company; National Bicycle Association; and United States Cycling Federation. **Climbing:** Frank Anderton, R.E.I. **Cross-Country Skiing:** Dave Gordan, Ski Hut; Kevin Washington, R.E.I.; Joyce Zinno, New Film Co.; Trak, Inc. **Downhill Skiing:** Kevin Washington, R.E.I.; Pam Drew and Gretchen Mariotti. **Exercising:** Skip Arroyo, Berkeley YMCA; Andrew and Jenny Gumperz. **Fishing:** C.J. McGowen and James David, Berkeley Bait and Tackle. **Frisbee Disc Playing:** Charles Tips, Dan Roddick, and the International Frisbee Association; **Gymnastics:** Ben Corr, Sportopia Gymnastics Center. **Ice**

Skating: Evelynne Gill, figure skating teacher at Berkeley Iceland; Jim David, general manager of Berkeley Minor Hockey Club; Manny Fernandez, Mano Foto. **Jogging:** Charles Tips, editor of *Running After 40*; Robert Burger, author of *Jogger's Catalog*. **Juggling:** John Cassidy, author of *Juggling for the Complete Klutz*; Bill Barr, director of the International Jugglers Association. **Martial Arts:** Alan Bultoch and Stefan Argent, Young's Trading Company; Roger Bliss. **Motorcycling:** Jim Rivera, Yamaha dealer; Scott Somers, Suzuki dealer; Linda Murphy, Motorcycle Safety Foundation; Robert Rasor, American Motorcyclist Association; Trisha Yeager, author of *How to be Sexy with Bugs in Your Teeth*. **Roller Skating:** Lee Cole and Jim Sniadach, Skates on Haight; Tom Cuthbertson. **Skateboarding:** Tom Cuthbertson; Judi Oyama, Santa Cruz Surf Shop; Robert Garrett, NHS, Inc. **Surfing:** Mike Duffy of O'Neill; Steve Pezman, *Surfer* Magazine; Jim Gordon. **Unicycling:** William Jenack of Jenack Cycles; Ray Caparros, Schwinn Bicycle Company. **Yo-Yo Playing:** Donald F. Duncan, Jr., and Dale Oliver, Duracraft, Inc.; Ben Baker, Duncan Yo-Yo Company; Tom Kuhn, Tom Kuhn Custom Yo-Yos.

This list would not be complete without also thanking all the teenagers in the photographs throughout the book, who were so eager to share their talents, and the people of Custom Process and Gersh Photo, who did such a fine job of processing and printing these photographs.

Last, but certainly not least, I would like to express my appreciation to the people who were there for me from the very beginning to the very end: my agent, Marcia Amsterdam; editors Louise Colligan, Ann Martin, and Dan Weiss; copy editor Mary–Katherine Kneip. Thank you all.

FOREWORD

If you've picked up *Getting Started In Solo Sports* to learn about some new fun activity that you can do on your own, then you're off to a good start. That's what this book is all about — helping you get into the game and started in solo sports. Whether you realize it or not, you're in the middle of a sports boom. Everywhere, people of all ages are becoming active — skating, bicycling, jogging, juggling, and participating in lots of other solo sports. With all these exciting things to do available to you, it's not easy to make choices. That's why I've written this book: to help you decide which activities are really the ones for you.

Before you invest a lot of time and money in buying equipment* and getting instruction, first read the chapter or chapters in this book that appeal to you. Read some of the books mentioned in the "Suggested Reading" at the end of each chapter section. Find out all that you can about the solo sports that interest you the most. Borrow or rent equipment and try out those areas of interest before you purchase expensive equipment. By following these suggestions, you will have what you need to get started. You will be equipped to make an intelligent decision, to select from all the solo sports available the ones you truly want to get involved in. Then, GO FOR IT! And, one last thing — HAVE FUN!

*The prices quoted throughout this book are approximate prices for 1981, and subject to change.

BACKPACKING

Getting Started

Anyone who has the desire, and is in good enough condition to carry his or her own equipment, is ready to start backpacking. Car camping and day hiking are excellent ways to prepare, but a common expression among seasoned backpackers is "The best conditioning for backpacking is backpacking."

Many beginning backpackers start with borrowed equipment. If you are starting out with borrowed items, then try them out on a short hike before your trip. Adjustments, like adding extra padding to the hip belt of your pack, are easy to make ahead of time, but nearly impossible once you hit the back country.

Renting equipment from a specialty backpacking or sporting goods store is an inexpensive way to get into backpacking. Before making major purchases, you can test out the equipment and find out your preferences.

Equipment

After a few backpacking adventures, you might decide to purchase some of your own equipment. Buying your own backpack is probably your best first investment—and the most important one. The fit and comfort of your pack can make or break your back and the back-packing trip! Whatever pack you choose to buy, make sure it has a padded hip belt and that all the straps feel comfortable. Relatively inexpensive, but excellent, packs are available from $50–$80. These packs are very basic, with welded aluminum frames and pack cloth of 100% nylon with waterproof coating, except for zippers and seams. (For total waterproofing, it is wise to purchase a pack cover. They cost anywhere from $13–$22.) Sturdy packs designed for young adults are manufactured by Camp Trails, Kelty, and Recreational Equipment, Inc. These are all good packs for people who are still growing. They will be usable for about four years.

When you've outgrown your first pack, or when you're ready to upgrade your equipment, more sophisticated packs are available. These packs cost more because they are made better, with better padding and more specialized features, like an ice ax holder or a crampon patch. More expensive packs cost anywhere from about $75–$165. Since there are lots of different packs to choose from, seek out the expert advice available at backpacking stores, or at sporting goods stores specializing in wilderness equipment. Many of these shops will take your old pack in on trade, or you can advertise it for sale on the shop's bulletin board.

When buying your first sleeping bag, look for a barrel-shaped one that's synthetic-filled and insulated. This type of bag is much less expensive than the prestigious down-filled bag, and can be purchased for as little as $50. More important, if it gets wet, you can wring it out and the bag still maintains its loft and warmth. A synthetic-filled bag will keep you warm to about freezing temperature. For lower temperatures and for winter camping, you'll need a bag with more sophisticated construction, with more insulation sewn through, and perhaps filled with down. These features will bring up the price substantially so that bags cost a minimum of about $80.

Most people want to start with a down-filled bag as they have been led to believe these are the "ultimate" in sleeping bags. But keep in mind, when a down bag gets wet, it's worthless until it dries out, which may take a couple of days. In addition, bags filled with down are often too warm for summer camping.

A common mistake of beginners is to start backpacking wearing tight, stiff, new hiking boots. As you hike along, the boots feel heavy and uncomfortable — much too much footwear for an easy trail. For the gentle hills and flat trails you will start hiking on, even a pair of old tennis shoes is preferable to poorly fitted hiking boots.

As you gain more backpacking experience, you will hike into more isolated areas where the trails become rougher and steeper, requiring a more supportive boot. At this point in your backpacking career, it's time to think about investing in a pair of good boots. But take a moment to evaluate your commitment to the sport. Are you going to make one more arduous trip and then store the boots in a closet until you've outgrown them? If you are seriously planning to continue backpacking, then you are ready to make this major purchase.

When it is finally time to buy, look for comfort and fit above all. Most good hiking boots are made with Vibram soles and good quality leather. Avoid boots with a large number of seams, because they may come apart later. All this may mean purchasing a more expensive boot. Remember, the boot has got to fit now or you've wasted your money. Quality hiking boots will cost anywhere from about $66–$110, so it pays to get fitted at a store that specializes in hiking boots.

Another item a backpacker eventually has to consider purchasing is some kind of shelter. The least expensive and quickest way to keep out some of the discomforts of wind, rain, sun, or insects is with a tube tent. A tube tent is a rectangular piece of plastic or coated nylon, about nine feet long and three feet wide at the base when erected, with the two opposite edges sealed together to form a tube. It can be rigged instantly by stringing a line through the tube and tying the ends about three feet above the ground to two supports. A sleeping bag holds down the floor, or it can be pegged down at the corners in bad weather. These "instant" tents cost anywhere from about $6–$28, and are available in one- or two-person sizes.

In wetter or colder climates, it's wise to borrow or rent a tent. Hundreds of variations of frame, tunnel, or dome-shaped nylon tents can also be purchased. The prices of tents are as varied as their shapes, ranging anywhere from

$35–$550, depending on size and construction.

As for planning menus and buying food for your trip, you might want the convenience of the slightly more expensive, prepackaged, one-pot, freeze-dried foods sold at special backpacking or mail-order food stores. Foods such as dried cereals, soups, and powdered milk, along with a host of other quick-cooking, lightweight, nutritious, and tasty products can also be found on supermarket shelves.

Cookware and eating utensils should be kept to a minimum. All you really need are a couple of old pots, a large coffee can, a plastic cup or Sierra cup, a pocket knife that doubles as an eating knife, and a tablespoon from the kitchen drawer.

A must for backpacking is a first-aid kit and handbook, and you would be wise to take a first-aid course before you attempt your first backpacking trip.

For a guide to other items you will need and how to pack them, the following checklist should prove helpful:

CHECKLIST

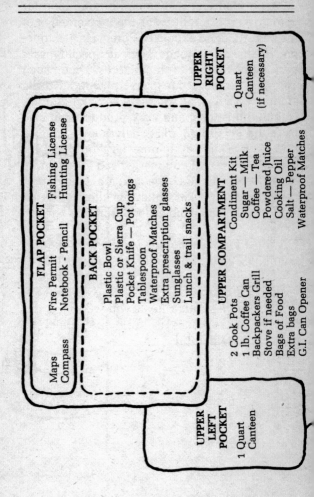

UPPER RIGHT POCKET

1 Quart Canteen (if necessary)

FLAP POCKET

Maps   Fire Permit   Fishing License
Compass   Notebook - Pencil   Hunting License

BACK POCKET

Plastic Bowl
Plastic or Sierra Cup
Pocket Knife — Pot tongs
Tablespoon
Waterproof Matches
Extra prescription glasses
Sunglasses
Lunch & trail snacks

UPPER COMPARTMENT

2 Cook Pots   Condiment Kit
1 lb. Coffee Can   Sugar — Milk
Backpackers Grill   Coffee — Tea
Stove if needed   Powdered Juice
Bags of Food   Cooking Oil
Extra bags   Salt — Pepper
G.I. Can Opener   Waterproof Matches

UPPER LEFT POCKET

1 Quart Canteen

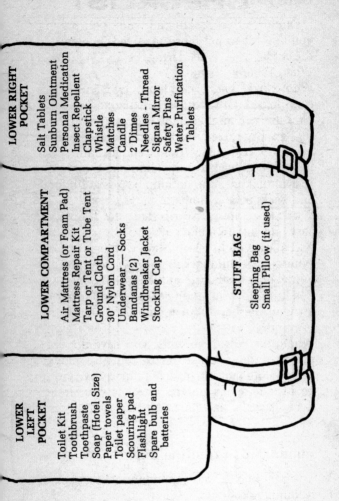

LOWER RIGHT POCKET

Salt Tablets
Sunburn Ointment
Personal Medication
Insect Repellent
Chapstick
Whistle
Matches
Candle
2 Dimes
Needles - Thread
Signal Mirror
Safety Pins
Water Purification Tablets

LOWER COMPARTMENT

Air Mattress (or Foam Pad)
Mattress Repair Kit
Tarp or Tent or Tube Tent
Ground Cloth
30' Nylon Cord
Underwear — Socks
Bandanas (2)
Windbreaker Jacket
Stocking Cap

STUFF BAG

Sleeping Bag
Small Pillow (if used)

LOWER LEFT POCKET

Toilet Kit
Toothbrush
Toothpaste
Soap (Hotel Size)
Paper towels
Toilet paper
Scouring pad
Flashlight
Spare bulb and batteries

(From *Backpacker's Sourcebook*, by P. Hargrove & N. Liebrenz, Berkeley: Wilderness Press, 1979.)

Getting Involved

Once you've assembled your equipment, you'll want to get more involved in planning the actual trip—considering the four W's: Who, What, Where, When.

Who: *Never* backpack alone. Solo wilderness camping is *only* for *very* experienced backpackers. You might decide to go with your family, an organized backpacking group, your Scout troop, or a few friends and an adult. Listings of local backpacking clubs and their activities often appear on bulletin boards at libraries and backpacking stores.

What: Keep your first trip short and simple, an easy one with room for change of route, one that will allow you to set up camp well before dark.

Where: In deciding where to go, you can consult guidebooks and trail guides (see "Suggested Reading"), or you might hear of a good trip from a friend. Perhaps your group leader has a trip in mind.

When: It's best to go when you have not only plenty of time to make the trip, but also enough time beforehand to plan it properly. When to go also depends on the weather you prefer. Every season has its particular camping rewards.

Inside Tips From the Experts

Gregg Mayer, an experienced backpacker, recommends:

1. Make your first trip an overnight: perhaps a base camp loop—one day in, one night sleepover, next day out.

2. Plan your clothing in layers, incorporating one garment made of wool, because wool retains most of its warmth even when wet.
3. *Carry a good first-aid kit and don't hit the trail without some basic first-aid training.*
4. Know your limits. Remember that the consequences of an accident are for more serious in the back country than at home.
5. When in the wilderness, remember the backpacker's credo: "Take only pictures, leave only footprints."
6. If you can carry it in full, you can carry it out empty. In other words, hold on to your cans, plastic containers, and other junk for proper disposal outside the wilderness area.

Suggested Reading

Hargrove, Penny and, Liebrenz, Noelle. *Backpacker's Sourcebook: A Book of Lists.* Berkeley: Wilderness Press, 1979.

Lyttle, Richard B. *The Complete Beginner's Guide to Backpacking.* New York: Doubleday and Co., 1975.

Standard First Aid and Personal Safety. New York: Doubleday and Co., 1977.

BICYCLING

Getting Started

You've more than likely done some bicycling. It's a rare teenager who hasn't already ridden either a one-speed coaster bike with a foot brake and balloon tires; a high-riser with raised handlebars, banana seat, and small wheels; or a sturdy, three-speed bike with a three-speed rear hub and caliper brakes front and back.

When you outgrow any of these bikes you may have ridden as a preteen, you'll probably want a free-wheel bicycle with hand brakes and ten speeds. These lightweight vehicles that look like racing bikes are more in demand today than any other type of bicycle. Nowadays, most teenagers prefer them because they make riding easier. With a ten-speed bike you can choose a gear ratio to match whatever riding conditions you meet: uphill, downhill, flat, fast, and slow. Furthermore, because these bikes are lightweight, riding long distances is less fatiguing. Many teenagers have become involved in bicycle motocross, or BMX, which requires yet another type of specialized bicycle designed for abuse on dirt roads and tracks.

Whatever bicycle you wish to ride, it's best to purchase it at a bicycle shop that specializes in the kind of bike you want. In the long run, you'll benefit from buying at a bike shop rather than a department or discount store. A bicycle dealer will give you a warranty on your new bike, customize it for you, make whatever adjustments might be necessary after you've owned it a short while, and service it regularly for you if you don't want to maintain it yourself.

Most bicycle dealers will also encourage you to sit on, or even ride, the bike you plan to buy to make sure it is not too big for you or that you're not too big for it. Charts that recommend certain sizes of frames according to height are, at best, approximations; they don't take into account people with long torsos and short legs or people with short torsos and long legs. You're the one who will be riding it, so make sure the bike feels comfortable to you. If you're between sizes or still growing, a bike dealer can judge whether you need the next size, or simply an adjustment to the seat or a longer seat post added to a smaller frame. In addition, a reputable bike dealer won't try to sell you the wrong bike for your size just because that's what he has in stock. *Riding a bike that's not the right size for you is not only uncomfortable, but can also be dangerous.*

Equipment

Sometimes you can purchase a used bicycle and save about fifteen percent of the cost of buying it new. But your choices are limited, and you run the risk of buying a bike that doesn't fit you or hasn't been properly cared for. If you do buy a secondhand bike, have it checked out by a good bike mechanic and have any worn parts replaced.

Selecting a new ten-speed from the hundreds of variations available can be an overwhelming task. As a rule, as the bikes get lighter, the features more refined and fancier, and the overall quality better, the price goes up, so that a ten-speed bicycle can cost anywhere from about $165–$1,100.

In the $165–$220 price range, a ten-speed bike is likely to have the following features: front quick-release hub, clincher tires with inner tube, seat post, racing handlebars, rims and frame of steel, and aluminum derailleur. They will weigh about 30–32 lbs.

In the $220–$275 price range are the "Continental ten-speeds" designed for women. They feature a "mixte" frame and upright, or touring, handlebars. The less expensive models in this group are made of the same materials as the men's bikes in the $165–$220 range and weigh about the same. The more expensive models may substitute aluminum rims for steel rims and weigh slightly less.

In the $275–$550 price range, ten-speed bikes generally have the following features: two quick-release hubs—front and back, all parts except the frame made from aluminum, and narrow clincher tires with inner tubes. These bikes usually weigh under 28 lbs.

In the highest price range, $550–$1,100, are the racing bikes, which have component parts of the finest quality, sew-up tires with an inner tube sewn in (no tools are required to change these tires as they are held to the rims with adhesive) and weigh under 22 lbs.

Accessories for ten-speed cycling include helmets—either a resistant shell made of hard impact plastic or the racing type made of padded leather straps. Both offer protection against abrasion and impact. Helmets range from about $11–$38. Shoes made especially for cyclists have a stiff sole and flexible upper which compresses the foot slightly so that the force of the pedal stroke keeps the bike moving forward. Shoes can cost anywhere from about $28–$66. Cycling shorts made of wool with a chamois crotch cost $28–$33. (In cold weather, wool

These bicycle racers wear a helmet made of padded leather straps for head protection. (Courtesy of Schwinn Bicycle Company)

tights or leg warmers are often worn by bicycle enthusiasts.) Bicycle jerseys with pockets in the back that won't restrict you while you cycle come with long or short sleeves and cost about $28–$38. Additional accessories for cycling include shoe cleats, toe clips, night lights, bike bags, horns, bells, chains, locks, mirrors, and fenders.

In motocross bikes, the least expensive and most basic, or stock, bike features a steel frame with 20-inch spoked steel wheels, all steel components, foot brake, soft vinyl seat, and rubber knobby tires. These bikes cost from $125–$155. For around $165, the frame and fork are made of chrome-molybdenum, while the rest of the components are steel. In the $187–$220 price range, steel wheels are replaced with aluminum-magnesium wheels ("mag" wheels) or colored plastic wheels. For around $220 a motocross bike can have the following features: an alloy hand brake system instead of a foot brake, aluminum alloy rims, tires in a multitude of colors—red, blue, or gold. Their weight is tremendously reduced because the tires are thinner and there is no foot brake. In the next price bracket, around $275, your BMX bike will come equipped with an all chrome-moly frame and cranks, forks and handlebars of light alloys, and an anodized-paint frame in brilliant colors. In the most expensive price range, about $330 and up, your motocross bike will be of the lightest weight, with all alloy components and a multicolored crank—an adaptation of the expensive ten-speed bike crank, which can be built completely to your specifications.

Once you've purchased even the basic, stock motocross bike, all parts except the frame can be upgraded. As you grow, longer seat posts can be added so you don't have to buy a whole new bike. BMX riders call making these modifications "tricking out" their bikes. Although BMX bikes have sturdier handlebars, frames, and wheels to begin with, riders and racers are continually replacing old or worn-out parts with better ones. Modifying a stock bike is part of the fun of motocross biking.

Accessories for motocross biking include padded covers for the bars to protect face and body from being injured when coming in contact with these bike parts, and helmets with chin straps for head protection. The helmets resemble those worn by motorcyclists and are made of hard impact plastic and styrofoam. Racers also wear long-sleeved shirts, face guards, goggles, and gloves, as well as elbow and chest pads. These items can be purchased at bike stores specializing in BMX bicycles.

Getting Involved

If you're the proud owner of a new ten-speed, you're itching to try it out, to take it for a spin. But where can you ride it? Since the bicycle boom of the 1970s, many towns and cities across the country have been busy planning and constructing bicycle routes, often through parks and other scenic areas, and also, where possible, on less traveled city streets. Your local Department of Transportation, Parks and Recreation, or Chamber of Commerce are the places to call

Cornering his BMX, #22 keeps just ahead of a pack of riders in this exciting motocross race. (Courtesy of Schwinn Bicycle Company)

for bicycling maps of your area. Local bicycle stores, bookstores, and libraries may have books that map out bicycle routes and rides in your region of the country. The authors, usually bicycle enthusiasts themselves, lay out quite a few scenic or interesting routes, tell the travel time for the average cyclist, mention their level of difficulty, and point out sights of interest along the routes.

More than likely there's a bicycle club where you live, or if there isn't, perhaps you can help to start one. Your local bike dealer will probably know how to put you in touch with the nearest bicycle club. Bike clubs organize group day rides, weekend outings, cross-country tours, bicycle races, and other recreational rides.

With your new motocross bike, you'll probably head for a vacant lot, dirt hills, or parks, looking for anything—even a sidewalk curb— to jump off. You'll want to try some wheelies, bunny hops, 180s, and kickouts. You may want to construct a simple wooden ramp for jumps.

Soon, you'll be looking for new challenges, and you'll want to race. Service clubs, such as the Rotary and Kiwanis, often sponsor races. Bike shops and city police or fire departments may also organize races.

If you do get into motocross racing, or even if you're just fooling around on some rugged back roads, *wear protective clothing and a helmet.*

Inside Tips From the Experts

Daniel Munch, a serious cyclist since the age of thirteen, recommends:

1. Use low gears when first learning how to ride a ten-speed bike.
2. Protect your bike from theft with a strong lock and chain made of hardened steel.
3. Make sure you have visible rear lights when riding at night.
4. Don't buy a bike that's too big for you.
5. If you ride in winter, dress warmly.
6. Be alert to surface conditions and traffic all around you.
7. Drive near the curb in the same direction as traffic. Always ride single file. Watch out for swinging car doors.
8. Avoid riding in wet weather if at all possible.
9. Keep bike tires in top condition.
10. Keep all parts properly adjusted and in good operating condition.
11. *As a cyclist you are the driver of a moving vehicle and must obey the same laws that govern motor traffic. Know these laws before your next bike ride.*

Suggested Reading

American Youth Hostel Handbook, American Youth Hostel, Inc., Delaplane, VA (lists youth hostels in U.S.A.).

Bicycling magazine, Emmaus, PA.

Scagnetti, Jack. *Bicycle Motocross*. New York: E. P. Dutton, 1976.

Sloane, Eugene. *The New Complete Book of Bicycling*. New York: Simon and Schuster, 1974.

CLIMBING

Getting Started

Any normal, healthy, young person in reasonably good physical and mental shape should be able to master the skills of rock climbing. If you have a naturally good sense of balance and are agile, or if you are involved in gymnastics, you may be at an advantage in learning this sport. Men, however, do not necessarily have an edge over women. Strength helps, but depending solely on strength develops bad habits in rock climbing. Anyone can learn to climb with agility, balance, and technique.

Rock climbing does not appeal to everyone. Some people can't adjust to the heights; others find it mentally tiring and physically exhausting to be continually looking for proper hand- and footholds. If, however, you are a person who likes to take risks, test your nerve, be challenged to the upper limits of your ability, and move up in the world (literally), then here's how to start rock climbing.

Despite all the advances in safety equipment, climbing is still considered a dangerous sport, and a beginner is always advised to proceed cautiously. Good climbers eventually avoid the daredevils of mountain climbing, because reckless climbers can get themselves and others hurt or even killed. Anyone seriously taking up rock climbing (and seriously is the only way to approach this sport) must first receive instruction and then practice all the climbing skills and safety precautions under expert supervision.

Organizations such as Outward Bound offer introductory courses in climbing. Some high schools, park services, and organized climbing clubs also have mountaineering programs. Rock climbing schools often advertise their services on bulletin boards in backpacking and mountaineering stores. Before you enroll, make sure the school is reputable.

In a series of lessons, rock climbing instructors will probably introduce you to climbing terminology, show you how to climb low angle rock, and then proceed to balance climbing and the principle of "three-point support" — having three points of your body in contact with the rock at all times. They will also teach you the basics of rope handling; belay, or using the rope as a safety device; and rappel, a rock maneuver that enables you to get down a cliff rapidly by means of a rope.

Along with lessons in the techniques of rock climbing, you must also learn how to be levelheaded, cool, courageous, team-spirited, and emotionally strong. Developing these personality traits are as essential to rock climbing as the equipment.

Equipment

Equipment is crucial in this sport; your life depends on it, so buy the best you can afford.

A young climber rappels down a rock face. (Wide World)

Basic rock climbing equipment includes ropes, rock climbing shoes, harness, safety helmet, and hardware. While you're in a class, you'll be borrowing much of this equipment; but if you plan to go on, you'll have to buy your own.

Probably the most important single piece of equipment is the rope. For beginners, the hawser rope, consisting of three strands of rope twisted together, is commonly used. Made from synthetic fibers and often referred to as goldline, this rope is less expensive than other types used in climbing, yet is safe and strong. It has one big advantage for beginners. You can easily inspect the fibers to see if they are damaged or frayed. Even if the rope is not worn, climbers usually buy a new one every year. They believe it's better to put an old rope than a climber to rest. Nowadays, the minimum rope length recommended for climbing is 150 feet. A goldline rope of this length costs anywhere from about $78–$100. Better ropes used by more advanced climbers for artificial climbing are known as kernmantel and are made of perlon. These cost $110–$132.

When you're starting out, you can wear tennis shoes or hiking boots; but if you plan to do more rock climbing, you will want to purchase specialized rock climbing shoes. These are narrow, with the welt cut in close to the boot. They are available in canvas, suede, or nylon uppers, and they generally have a high top and a thin, smooth, rubber sole. They should fit snugly. Have a salesperson who knows something about climbing shoes (preferably one who has done some climbing) help you choose your shoes.

They will cost anywhere from $55–$88.

Another important item for the serious beginner is a safety helmet. These helmets look like hardhats and cost about $28–$55. The less expensive ones are usually made of fiberglass and the more expensive ones of lexan, which is the material used in the astronauts' helmets because it is light, yet strong. Make sure the helmet you buy has a chin strap.

As you become more acquainted with what kind of climbing you want to do, you will build up a rack, which is an assortment of hardware on a sling, consisting of carabiners (artificial aids for rock climbing) and various sizes of protective devices: hexagonal nuts or "hexes," pitons, t-tons, and cam nuts. These purchases should be delayed, however, until your level of ability calls for them.

To further protect the climber in the event of a fall, the rope is attached to a harness. This piece of equipment is made out of nylon webbing, the same material used in seat belts, and can cost anywhere from about $6 (for one you can make yourself) to $66 (for a harness worn over the chest and waist). Clothing worn by climbers should be protective and durable. Gloves are often worn to prevent rope burn.

Getting Involved

After you've learned and practiced the basics of rock climbing, becoming a climber is all up to you. Perhaps you'll want to start climbing at your present level of ability, and then, after a year or so, get more instruction. Climbing is a team effort, so you'll need to choose a partner, someone you trust and feel good about. Don't start climbing with someone who has a "Go for it!" attitude. Perhaps there's someone in your climbing school, class, club, or troop with whom you'd like to climb.

Once you've chosen a partner, you can do some practice climbs together: some bouldering, some short climbs of one or two pitches (a pitch is the distance a climber has to travel from one belay to another), and a few day climbs (returning home or to a base camp at the end of your outing).

When you're ready for more challenging activity, most mountain clubs organize harder climbs, graded according to difficulty and led by either a certified or experienced mountain climber. *Whenever you climb, tell a friend or someone at home where you are going, your route, and when to expect you back.*

Inside Tips From the Experts

Frank Anderton, experienced salesperson of mountaineering equipment, passes on these tips to beginning climbers:

1. *Never climb alone.*
2. Know your equipment and its limits.
3. Stay relaxed and levelheaded.
4. Know when to finish a climb. Don't try to finish one that shouldn't be finished. Even experienced climbers back off a climb before it finishes them.
5. If you're going to climb, take it seriously. A

whole magazine entitled *Accidents In North American Mountaineering* is published annually.

Suggested Reading

Smith, Howard, E. *The Complete Beginner's Guide to Mountain Climbing.* New York: Doubleday and Co., 1977.

Wilkerson, James, A., M.D. *Medicine For Mountaineering.* Seattle: The Mountaineers, 1975.

Wheelock, Walt. *Ropes, Knots and Slings For Climbers.* Glendale, CA: La Siesta Press, 1967.

CROSS-
COUNTRY
SKIING

Cross-country skiing — also known as X-C, Nordic skiing, and ski touring — is the sport of gliding across stretches of snow with skis and poles under your own power. Unlike downhill skiing, which takes place at a designated ski area, cross-country skiing, as its name suggests, allows you to explore and appreciate the natural beauty of the winter landscape, free of ski lifts, snow equipment and crowds of other skiers.

Getting Started

X-C ski enthusiasts agree that if you're old enough to walk, you can learn how to ski tour; young and old alike can equally enjoy it. You don't have to be in any special physical condition to engage in this sport. Most important, the fundamentals of X-C skiing can be learned in a very short time; you'll probably be moving about on your touring skis after your very first lesson.

If you're a beginner and no one is available to teach you the basics, you'll find that the most worthwhile lessons are those offered at one of the several hundred ski touring centers throughout the United States and Canada. The large touring centers offer extensive lessons for skiers of all abilities, prepare and maintain trails, rent equipment, and may even send out radio-equipped ski patrols.

X-C ski instructors will start out by teaching you such basics as how to get into your skis, how to grip the poles, and how to make the diagonal stride (which is simply walking forward on skis). Eventually you will have to learn how to change direction, and you will be taught basic turns like the step and the snowplow. At some point you will also be introduced to the uphill stride and straight downhill skiing. Since it's more than likely you'll fall at some time or other, you'll learn early in your lessons how to fall and how to get up properly. Although you can progress quite rapidly from beginner to intermediate skier, the challenge of this sport comes in perfecting your rhythm and the smoothness of your strides and turns, as well as increasing your endurance and distance. Becoming an expert Nordic skier can take years of practice.

Equipment

The best advice anyone can give you in cross-country skiing is to tell you what to wear. Nothing can make you more miserable your first time out than being too warm or too cold. You will more than likely be able to wear some items you already own. Woolen pants, socks, gloves, mittens, sweaters, and hats are highly recommended; wool retains body heat even when wet.

Woolen pants, socks, gloves, mittens, and hats are highly recommended for cross-country skiing, as wool retains body heat even when wet. (Photo by Christopher G. Knight, TRAK, Inc.)

When you are first learning, you'll probably fall more than occasionally, so don't make the mistake of wearing jeans. When they get wet, they offer no protection against chill. Surplus army and navy stores sell woolen army pants at a low price. When cut down, they make excellent, loose-fitting knickers. Since ski touring is a very active sport, it's best to wear several layers of light wool clothing that allow you to move freely. Then, as your body generates heat, you can shed a layer of clothing before you get overheated; and if you start feeling cold, you can add a sweater or windbreaker. To keep snow out of your boots, you may have to purchase nylon gaiters, which are worn around the ankles. It's a good idea to go to a reliable ski shop and inquire about what kind of clothing to wear.

Before you purchase the basic equipment for X-C skiing, it's best to rent it to find out if you really are interested enough in the sport to make some initial purchases in the $110–$220 range. If cross-country skiing is the sport for you, there are a few ways to save some money when you decide to buy your own equipment. You may be able to get a good set of rental skis when they go on sale at ski shops at the end of the season, or you can purchase last year's models when the ski season is over. Some large, reputable ski shops offer a quality beginner's package that includes skis, boots, poles, bindings, and mounting for $110–$165.

Today, touring classes start 99% of beginners on waxless, lightweight touring skis. When you're ready to buy, you should consider purchasing this type of ski, for the following reason.

Waxless X-C skis allow you to spend time developing your skiing technique without having to worry about whether you are waxing your skis properly. Later on, when your ability improves, you may want to purchase more advanced skis. Then you can decide between waxless and waxed. At that point you can also enroll in a waxing clinic (offered at most ski shops during the season) and learn correct waxing techniques.

If you don't buy your equipment in a package, skis can run anywhere from about $82–$176. In years past, all X-C skis were made of laminated layers of wood, but today touring skis are also constructed of fiberglass, foam, and plastic.

To determine the right length of ski for you, simply raise your arm above your head with your fingers outstretched, and stand a ski on the floor. The tip of the ski should come to the bend in your wrist. A reliable ski salesperson will also take your weight into consideration when helping you choose the right skis.

Your boots should fit you like street shoes. Boots run from about $18–$82. The less expensive boots are constructed of synthetic materials. Leather that has been waterproofed is used for the more expensive boots.

Poles cost anywhere from $11–$82, but the cheaper poles made out of cane are still preferred over the more expensive aluminum and fiberglass poles now available. As for selecting bindings and mounting them on your skis, it's best to trust the ski shop to set them up to fit your boots.

Getting Involved

If you live in an area where there's snow in winter, getting involved is as easy as stepping out the door. You can practice ski touring on just about any snow-covered surface: your own backyard, public parks, golf courses, hiking trails, snow-covered meadows and forests, and even jogging and bicycle paths.

If you have to travel to the snow and head to a ski touring center, the trip is well worth it. You'll soon find yourself in a woodland environment, surrounded by crisp, unpolluted air and snow, away from the noise and crowds of civilization. Once you're touring, it won't take you long to realize that one of the greatest joys of cross-country skiing is discovering a new world of freedom and beauty. Good places to go ski touring are listed in ski magazines and directories (see "Suggested Reading") and at local ski shops.

Another advantage of ski touring is that it can be enjoyed by the whole family. All the members of your family can ski on the same terrain and at a pace everyone can handle. Parents and kids don't have to split up and head for different slopes as they do in downhill skiing. For an outdoor, family sport that is simple to learn and relatively inexpensive (once the initial equipment is rented or purchased), cross-country skiing is hard to beat!

Inside Tips From the Experts

Dave Gordan and Kevin Washington, both experienced X-C skiers, agree on the following tips for first-time skiers:

1. Rent before you buy.
2. The importance of early lessons cannot be overemphasized. Bad habits are hard to correct.
3. Wear wool clothing; we can't stress that enough.
4. Buy your equipment at a reputable ski shop.
5. It's more important to use a good sunscreen in the snow than at the beach.
6. Wear sunglasses or goggles for eye protection. Sunlight reflected off the snow can be extremely bright.

Suggested Reading

Caldwell, John. *The Cross-Country Ski Book*. Brattleboro, VT: The Stephen Greene Press, 1981.

Gillette, Ned. *Cross-Country Skiing*. Seattle: The Mountaineers, 1979.

Nordic Skiing, Nordic Skiing Inc., West Brattleboro, VT.

Skiers Directory, Ski Earth Publications, Inc., Boston, MA.

DOWNHILL
SKIING

Getting Started

Getting started with good equipment that's within your budget can present you with more challenges than your first trip down the bunny slopes. These days, trying to outfit yourself in new ski equipment while you're still growing is expensive. Foot growth charts indicate that young people from twelve to fifteen years of age need new shoes every sixteen to twenty weeks. So renting equipment from your local ski shop is highly recommended for teens. It's also a good idea to rent the equipment before your ski trip rather than when you get to the ski area. Renting locally will allow you more time to be properly fitted in boots and skis (with less risk of the rental shop being out of your size) and more skiing time when you get to the slopes.

Finding a pair of boots that fits you well is probably the most important, but often the most difficult, task in renting equipment. Rental boots are just not made as well as the boots for sale. It's best to shop for boots to rent in the same way you would shop to buy. Wear a pair of ski socks when trying on boots. Don't be satisfied with the rental boots available in one ski shop. Look around in several shops for the boots that feel most comfortable. They should fit snugly around the heel without pinching your foot, with a little room in front to wiggle your toes. You may end up renting your boots at one shop and your skis and poles at another. But it's worth the extra trouble to avoid having to spend six to eight hours on the slopes in boots that hurt your feet. Once you've found comfortable rental boots, stick with them, and experiment, if you like, with renting different types and lengths of skis and poles. Experienced personnel at good rental ski shops will match your skis and poles to your size.

Once you've rented your equipment, you should start thinking about what to wear when you go skiing. You can downhill ski in just about anything, even your jeans or overalls as many teenagers do, but you will keep warmer and drier if you wear nylon powder pants (ski pants) or waterproof stretch pants with thermal underwear under them. As for a jacket, your own winter jacket or down parka will probably fit the bill, as long as it's warm, wind-resistant, and if possible, waterproof. For a day or weekend of skiing, you can waterproof your jacket and jeans with a can of inexpensive waterproof spray. It's highly recommended to invest in a wool hat and ski socks, if you don't already own them, and padded leather ski gloves or mittens. In downhill skiing, you won't be generating as much body heat as in X-C skiing and your body will be cooling down as you wait on lift lines, so dress warmly in layers with a wool sweater and turtleneck jersey under your jacket. When you ski, you should always apply a sunscreen cream to your face and wear sunglasses or goggles. The sun's rays in the mountains combined with reflection from the snow can severely injure your eyes and skin if they are not properly protected.

Clothes designed especially for downhill skiing are appealing because they offer more freedom of movement, are made of wind- and water-repellent fabrics, and certainly make you look and feel in style; but resist the temptation to buy them until you're sure that skiing is your sport and that you're on your way to becoming an accomplished skier.

To help you learn or improve, ski resorts all over the country run ski schools that offer classes graded according to your ability. Enrolling in a ski school class is the best way to learn how to ski. All ski instructors are required by the Professional Ski Instructors Association to spend two to four years learning how to teach skiing to people of all ages. Today many ski schools use two relatively new teaching techniques: the Graduated Length Method, where you start out on short skis and graduate to longer ones, and the American Teaching Method, which emphasizes a natural style of skiing while learning the basic skills. Using either of these two methods, rather than the traditional European teaching methods, simplifies learning and gives you confidence and control early in your lessons. Ski schools across the nation are attempting to standardize their instruction. Until this is accomplished, it's best to stick with one school and one teaching approach to avoid confusion when you are first learning.

No matter what teaching method you choose or where you take lessons, the goals of a good ski instructor should be to teach you, the beginner, how to carry your skis and poles; get in and out of your equipment; use your body, skis, and poles to keep balanced; walk uphill, ski downhill, make turns, stop, get up from a fall, and be in control at all times. You'll also be taught how to get on and off ski lifts without injuring yourself and others, and you'll learn the traffic safety rules of downhill skiing.

If you already know how to cross-country ski, you'll probably be able to apply many of the techniques of that sport to downhill skiing and move beyond the basics that much sooner.

If skiing is an entirely new sport for you, the benefits of early lessons in a ski school cannot be overemphasized. Books and magazine articles on how to ski can reinforce and refine what you've learned in your ski class, but written instruction cannot replace the expert attention and direction you'll get from a trained ski instructor at a ski school.

Equipment

After renting your equipment a few times, you'll probably be tempted to buy some of your own. Here again, it must be said that it's wise to put off these expensive purchases until you've stopped growing. But if you feel you must have your own—and can afford it—it's a good idea to put most of your money into an excellent pair of boots. That same amount of money spent trying to buy skis, boots, poles, and bindings will get you only the cheapest equipment—which will not hold up to the rigors of downhill skiing.

A good pair of boots made of the most modern materials—a polyplastic outer shell with an inner boot of polyurethane foam—costs anywhere from $55–$220. For such a big investment, you must get properly fitted at a specialty ski shop where the salespeople know how to help you select the best-fitting boot for your skiing needs. Whichever one you finally choose, don't buy a pair of boots that doesn't meet the D. I. N. (Deutsche Industrie Normen) 7880 standard for boot sole configuration. This standard, stamped on the boot, insures that the boot surfaces which must interface with a ski binding will fit virtually any set of bindings on skis manufactured today.

It's risky to buy old, used boots or skis at ski swaps or from friends. Beside being worn out, the equipment may be out-of-date and no longer considered functional by the ski shops that have to service this equipment. If you can't resist searching for a bargain at a ski swap, take someone with you who is familiar with today's equipment, or attend a ski swap at a ski shop where there are sales personnel present who can make expert recommendations about the equipment you are thinking of buying. Ski swaps are good places to pick up bargains in ski clothes, such as powder pants, jackets, sweaters, long underwear, turtleneck jerseys, hats, and gloves.

Since a good pair of skis can cost anywhere from about $110 up, and you'll probably have to buy a new pair of boots almost every season, you'll be better off to continue renting your skis and poles until you've stopped growing. Then you can put the money saved into buying a better boot. Look around for a shop that offers you credit on the purchase of new boots when you trade in the ones you've outgrown.

Getting Involved

When you're ready to go skiing, local ski shops can advise you on which resorts cater to families, groups, or solo skiers; which areas run ski school programs and rent equipment; and which ski resorts in your region would best suit your needs. Ski magazines and regional ski news publications put out by the regional offices of the United States Ski Association also publish information on where to go skiing. Thanks to the development of modern snow-making machinery, 35 out of the 50 states now boast resorts. If getting to one of them is a problem for you, ski clubs, schools, and Y's often organize day and weekend outings to the snow. Local ski shops can also help you link up with a ski group.

When you arrive at a ski area, check the resort's information desk for where you can rent equipment and take lessons and where emergency facilities, telephones, and restrooms are located. Be sure to ask which trails are best for you to ski at your present level of ability. You can also call any of the ski resorts beforehand to find out what particular services and facilities they offer. The more planning you do before your ski trip, the more fun you'll have once you get there!

Inside Tips From the Experts

Here are some tips from Kevin Washington, an experienced ski equipment salesperson. Following these suggestions makes good sense for skiers of all abilities.

1. Make all the effort you can to keep your equipment in top shape and to maintain it. Don't walk through parking lots or on concrete with your ski boots. If you own your own skis, have the bindings checked once a year. When you travel, protect them with ski bags or a binding cover. Keep your skis tuned. Ski shops perform this service or will teach you how to do it yourself in ski clinics.

2. Ski only when in control. Don't ski when overly tired or injured.

3. When you locate rental equipment you like, write down where you rented it and any identifying numbers on the equipment, so you can rent the same equipment the next time.

4. Stay on groomed and marked trails when skiing. Move quickly out of runout areas at the top of lifts and the bottom of runs.

5. Read up on special pre-skiing conditioning exercises. Work up a program for yourself that includes muscle stretching and flexing exercises and do them regularly for two to three months prior to your ski trip.

6. Don't ski in blizzards or any type of bad weather.

7. Watch out for symptoms of frostbite—white patches on areas ordinarily pink; and tin-

gling, pain, or numbness in any part of the body, especially the extremities.

8. Look at a map of the ski area and ski only where you belong according to your ability.

9. Even if you're beyond the beginner's stage, enrolling in an intermediate or advanced lesson can be beneficial. Virtually all skiers, even experts, can learn to ski better.

10. Bring your own lunch, including a hot beverage, and avoid crowds and high prices at ski resorts' cafeterias.

Suggested Reading

Lyttle, Richard. *The Complete Guide to Skiing.* New York: Cornerstone Library, Simon and Schuster, 1979.

D. Needham, ed. *Ski Magazine's Encyclopedia of Skiing.* New York: Harper and Row, 1979.

Skiing magazine, New York, NY.

EXERCISING

Getting Started

The first, but often the hardest, step in getting started in an exercise program is deciding to exercise. To make it easier and more enjoyable, you may want to encourage a friend or your entire family to exercise with you, or you might try exercising to music.

Next, from hundreds of different exercises, you must select the ones that meet your needs. If being more flexible and moving with ease is your goal, you might choose such exercises as yoga, calisthenics, or any program involving bending, stretching, and rotating parts of the body. For gaining strength, developing and toning muscles, and for general body building, you may select a fitness program that involves the use of weights, push-ups, press-ups, sit-ups, and squatting movements. Aerobic or "with air" exercises such as jumping rope, skipping, and jogging will improve your overall fitness, endurance, and the performance of your heart and lungs. Anyone can benefit from this type of exercise.

You may decide to take up a new activity such as cross-country skiing, jogging, or tennis, all of which are excellent forms of exercise. Every sport has a specific set of exercises for pre-conditioning, warm-up, and post-conditioning that stretch, flex, and strengthen the muscles you will use. If you're just beginning, it's essential to choose an exercise program that properly prepares you for participation in your new sport. If you are already active in a particular sport, find out what exercises will help to improve your performance. Athletes who train regularly in addition to practicing their sport have a definite advantage over athletes who do not train. Whether or not you're athletic, if you exercise routinely—no matter what series of exercises you choose—you will be in better physical condition and probably lead a longer, healthier, and more active life.

Getting Involved

Once you've made the decision to exercise and have chosen the fitness program best suited for you (see "Suggested Reading"), check your schedule and determine a time in the day when you can exercise regularly. Setting aside a specific time just for exercising will help make exercise a part of your daily routine. This period in your day can be anywhere from five to forty-five minutes—or longer, depending on your schedule, on the exercise program you're involved in, and your present level of health and fitness. (Even if you think you are healthy, but especially if you have any specific health problems, be sure to check with your physician before beginning any physical fitness program.) Exercise in a place that is comfortable and where there are not too many distractions. If you need to exercise with others, choose a time and place that's convenient for all of you. Sometimes enrolling in a class at a local Y, school, or recreation center will help you keep up your interest and introduce you to some new exercises, as well as to some new friends to share them with.

Follow your exercise program as closely as you can. Most fitness programs start you off gently and increase the levels of performance gradually, so don't go all out the first day. If you get tired, stop and rest before continuing, or stop altogether. If you become ill, don't exercise. When you are well again, begin at a lower level than where you left off and don't overdo it.

Keep in mind that regular exercise of any kind requires time and effort. Once you choose a program, work at it with a positive attitude, be patient with yourself, start slowly and carefully, gradually increasing your effort, and you'll soon find yourself feeling more physically fit and in better condition for whatever else you want to do.

Inside Tips From the Experts

Skip Arroyo, director of the Berkeley YMCA Physical Fitness Center, offers the following tips to teenagers involved in exercising:

1. Deep breathing is the most important part of any exercise. Check your specific program for correct breathing techniques.
2. Drink lots of water every day.
3. Be aware of your total food intake and the types of food you eat each day. Too much

sugar? Too many soft drinks? French fries? corn chips? potato chips? Cracker Jacks?

4. Don't overdo it. Slow and steady is the best way to exercise.

5. Include some form of relaxation or winding down at the end of each exercise session.

6. Develop a daily routine that includes warm-up, exercise, and relaxation—and stick to it!

Suggested Reading

Englebardt, Stanley. *How To Get In Shape For Sports*. New York: Lothrop, Lee, and Shepard Co., 1976.

Myers, Clayton. *The Official YMCA Physical Fitness Handbook*. New York: Popular Library, 1975.

The Diagram Group, ed. *The Complete Encyclopedia of Exercises*. New York and London: Paddington Press, 1979.

FISHING

Getting Started

There's no correct age for fishing; you can take up the sport at five, fifteen, or fifty. About one out of three Americans try fishing at some time. You may have tried it already, but if you haven't, here's how you can get started.

The first step you need to take before outfitting yourself with any type of fishing gear is to find out what kinds of fish you're likely to find in your locale, and in what kinds of water. If you live in one of the coastal states, you might consider taking up ocean fishing, which requires saltwater fishing tackle. Your state may have good fishing in its lakes, rivers, or streams and that requires freshwater fishing equipment. Your local bait and tackle store can tell you what fish are available near you and what tackle to purchase. Every state has a Fish and Game Department which publishes literature describing the fishing waters in your state. Take this information into consideration when selecting your rod and reel.

Your Fish and Game Department also publishes information on the fishing regulations in your state, any limits on fishing in its waters, and at what age you will need to get a fishing license. Before you go fishing, be sure you know all these regulations, and get your license if your state requires it. By writing to the Fish and Game Department in the state capital, you can get a copy of the fishing regulations. Or your local sporting goods stores and tackle shops may have copies on hand.

Another important resource that can be purchased at your local tackle shop is a fishing map. On these maps are clearly marked all the reservoirs, ponds, lakes, rivers, streams, and oceans that can be fished in your region of the country.

Once you've decided where you want to go fishing, put off buying your bait until you're there. Local bait shops are more likely to carry the bait you'll need for catching the particular fish in nearby waters, and the fishermen there will be able to advise you on what bait to use.

All the books and pamphlets in the world on fishing won't teach you as much about how to fish as practice and experience will, especially if you go fishing your first few times with a more experienced fisherman.

Equipment

With fishing tackle, like most other types of sports equipment, buy the best your budget will allow. But if you can only spend a few dollars, don't give up fishing. Buy an inexpensive plastic pole, some line, leaders, hooks, plastic bobbers, sinkers, and bait — and go bobber fishing!

If you can afford to spend a little more, then look for a complete fishing outfit in the blister-pack promotional packages put out by major fishing tackle manufacturers. These prepackaged outfits often go on sale around Christmas and before the fishing season opens. You might even find them on sale in discount, department, or drug stores, so shop around. A complete set for freshwater fishing — which includes a rod, reel, line, lead shot, and hooks — will cost around $27. The same type set for saltwater fishing will run around $50.

If you can afford better-quality equipment, then buy the component parts separately. A quality reel for freshwater fishing can cost anywhere from about $27-$138, the rod $20-$275 and the line 3¢ to 10¢ a yard. The salesperson at your local sporting goods store should be able to help you match your gear to the type of fishing you will be doing most often.

For a multipurpose freshwater fishing outfit, your best bet is probably an open-face spinning reel of medium size with removable spool; and a collapsible, two-piece, fiberglass rod, 6 to 7 feet in length with medium action. Your line should be nylon monofilament with 6- to 10-pound test. For saltwater fishing, you should be looking at heavier equipment, with basically the same features as for freshwater, and a rod 7 to 10 feet in length. Your line will be heavier with 15- to 20-pound test. No matter what equipment you choose, the salesperson should help you assemble it and give you some tips on how to use it properly.

Don't forget to buy a tackle box or bag and a stringer for holding the fish you catch. Each time you go fishing, you will probably add a piece of equipment to your tackle box; a new lure, a set of hooks, or a sinker. Before you know it, you'll be well equipped for catching a variety of fish.

Getting Involved

One of the best ways to learn how to fish is to tag along with an experienced fisherman and observe his fishing techniques. If you don't know anyone who can teach you, go to a local pier, stream, or lake and watch other fishermen.

Often Park and Recreation Departments run casting clinics. Your local tackle shop may also know of a casting or fishing club. Most often these classes are free. Once you learn the basic casts — the snap and the lob — you can practice them in a backyard swimming pool or local pond or lake. Hula hoops and garbage can lids floating in the water make excellent casting targets. *Remember to look behind you before you cast.*

Although there is a fee charged for a day's fishing, an outing on a fishing or party boat can't be beat for learning how to catch saltwater fish. Often the equipment is supplied and the captain will take you out to the action. Experienced fishermen will be on board to help you. More than likely, you'll come home with your fair share of the day's catch.

Eventually, baiting your hook, dropping or casting your line, and waiting to catch a fish will no longer present you with a challenge. You will want to match your fishing skill and knowledge to a particular fish. At this point you will need to learn some very specific fishing techniques such as fly fishing, and purchase some specialized equipment. Before you make any purchases, ask yourself, "What types of fish interest me the most? In what waters do I like to fish? What fishing methods will I be using?" The answers to these questions will help your salesperson match the equipment you buy to your particular fishing preferences.

There are many fishermen today who will be quick to tell you that no matter what equipment you use, there's more to fishing than catching fish. They'll talk of the simple pleasures: being outdoors in the sun; observing animal, plant, and marine life; and, at last, the satisfaction of bagging your own food and bringing it home. When you experience catching your first fish, you too may be hooked on the sport!

Inside Tips From the Experts

Here are some fishing tips that trophied fishermen would want to pass on to those just starting out.

1. Avoid disturbing the waters of other fishermen. Give them the "stretch of the river," which is the farthest distance they can cast.
2. When you get good enough, don't feel you have to go home with your limit. Catch and release some of your fish. To release them unharmed, follow these steps:
   a. Never squeeze the fish hard.
   b. Never touch the gills.
   c. If the hook cannot be easily removed, cut the leader and leave the hook in place.
   d. If the fish is exhausted, hold it in an upright position in the water and move it gently back and forth until it swims away.

   e. Use a barbless hook to aid in the release
     of the fish.

There's glory in catching and then releasing some of your fish to provide recreation for another day!

3. Know the limits and other regulations of the waters you are fishing.
4. Look behind you before you cast.
5. Approach fishing waters slowly and quietly.
6. Check your local newspaper for a column on fishing. The outdoors columnist may tell you where the best fishing is that week, what bait to use, and what fish you will catch.

Suggested Reading

Fabian, John. *Fishing For Beginners.* New York: Atheneum, 1977.

McClane, A. J. *Secrets of Successful Fishing.* New York: Holt, Rinehart, and Winston, 1979.

Consumer Guide, ed. *Whole Fishing Catalog.* New York: Simon and Schuster, 1978.

FRISBEE DISC PLAYING

Getting Started

Nothing could be easier than getting started in Frisbee disc play. Simply find a willing friend and an open space in a park, schoolyard, backyard, field, or beach and begin throwing your Frisbee disc. It's a good idea to start tossing it back and forth slowly to avoid straining and spraining your shoulder, arm, hand, or leg muscles; don't overdo throwing your disc the first time out.

If you're just learning, there are basic grips, throws, and catches you'll want to master: the backhand or common grip, with the thumb on top and the rest of the fingers hooked under the disc; the backhand, underhand, curve, and skip shot throws; and the one-handed catch where the disc is caught in the natural pocket between the thumb and index finger. There are lots of good books available that fully describe these beginning techniques (see "Suggested Reading").

If no partner is around to help you perfect these basics, you can practice in several other ways. Start by practicing your throws against a sturdy wall, like a tennis backboard. To improve your accuracy, set up a target and try to throw your disc through it. By hanging a Hula-Hoop or a cardboard ring between two posts about 3 feet off the ground, you can construct an upright, stationery target. Stand about 10 yards away and try to throw your disc through the hoop. As your throws become more accurate, increase your distance from the target. You can throw your Frisbee disc for distance; throw, run, and catch it (TRC) as far as possible from the spot you originally tossed it; or time how long you can keep it in flight. Throwing for accuracy, distance, and maximum time aloft (MTA) are part of established field events in Frisbee disc tournaments. With enough practice, maybe you'll break some Frisbee disc world records!

Getting Involved

Once you've mastered the beginning techniques, you'll be ready for some trick throws, fancy flips, and creative catches: the sidearm, roller, hover, and boomerang throws; the overhand wrist and thumb flips; the behind-the-head, behind-the-back, between-the-leg catches; one-finger and knee tips; and nail delays.

You can do some freestyle throwing and catching by playing some simple Frisbee disc games. With two people you can practice your repertoire in a game of catch. In Follow the Leader you throw the disc any way you want to and your partner has to imitate your throw; in turn, you must repeat his catch. With more players, you can "hot dog" the disc around in a circle as fast as possible in a game of Sweet

A Frisbee disc expert makes a spectacular under-the-leg catch. (Courtesy of the International Frisbee® Association®)

Georgia Brown. In Keepaway the object is to prevent a person in the center of a circle of players from catching the Frisbee disc as the others throw it back and forth. To add to the fun, the person in the middle may use his own disc to intercept or knock down the other players' throws. Take any sport you can think of and play it with a Frisbee disc: Frisbee football, Frisbee baseball, Frisbee basketball, and target games. Frisbee disc play is limited only by your imagination, so be inventive and make up your own games.

More involved games include Frisbee golf, Guts Frisbee, and Ultimate Frisbee. In Frisbee golf there are tee areas, hazards, and targets for "holing out"—such as baskets and specially designed disc pole-holes. In some parks across the country, there are even permanent Frisbee golf courses. But part of the fun of Frisbee golf is laying out your own course.

Guts Frisbee is a disc sport with one to five players on a team. Each team lines up along parallel goal lines about 16 yards apart. The object of Guts is to throw the Frisbee disc so hard and fast that the receiving team cannot make a good one-handed catch. If the throw is not caught, the throwing team receives one point. The winning team is the one that first stacks up 21 points, winning by a 2-point lead.

Ultimate Frisbee is a non-contact field sport played by two 7-person teams on a 40- to 60-yard playing field. The object of the game is to score a goal by successfully passing the disc to a member of your team in the other team's end zone. At the end of a 48-minute time period, the team with the most points is declared the winner.

Equipment

Although there are a few other manufacturers of quality discs, those made by Wham-O are the best available. Their current line includes ten different models ranging in price from about $1.75 for the regular model to about $5.50 for the top of the line, the 165G World Class Frisbee Disc. Charles Tips, author of *Frisbee Sports and Games*, recommends the World Class Frisbee 97G for anyone thirteen or under. For players thirteen and up, he suggests models 119G, 141G, or the Super Pro. No matter what Wham-O disc you choose, Tips says, "It pays to buy a quality disc because they fly truer."

Inside Tips From Tips

Charles Tips offers the following tips to beginning Frisbee disc players:

1. To make successful backhand throws, the trick is to lead with your elbow and let your wrist cock as it comes straight through. This method of throwing makes your throws straighter and more accurate; it also gives them more spin.

2. Practice this technique by standing facing a wall and throwing the disc so that it touches the wall all the way through the throw.

3. An overhand throw is simple. After catching your Frisbee disc with your thumb on bottom

and your fingers on top, cock the disc down
on top of your forearm, bring your arm back,
then swing your arm forward, shoulder high,
to make the throw.
4. The most fun in Frisbee disc play is invent-
ing catches of your own — behind your back,
lying down, running, even trapping it between your knees. The trick to successful
catches is to wait until the last second to
make your move.
5. Any Frisbee disc game can be played indoors
without knocking over lamps if you use a
Mini-Frisbee. On rainy days you can still
play great games of Guts Frisbee, freestyle
throwing and catching, and Frisbee golf.

Suggested Reading

Norton, Goldy. *The Official Frisbee Handbook.*
New York: Bantam Books, 1972.

Poynter, Margaret. *Frisbee Fun.* New York: Julian Messner, 1977.

Tips, Charles. *Frisbee Disc Sports and Games.*
Millbrae, CA: Celestial Arts, 1979.

Tips, Charles. *Frisbee by the Masters.* Millbrae,
CA: Celestial Arts, 1979.

GYMNASTICS

Getting Started

There's no right age to get started in gymnastics, but a general rule is the younger, the better. If you haven't begun training at the early ages of five, six, or seven, another good time to begin gymnastics—especially if you're a young woman—is in your early teens, when your body weight is well proportioned and you're still light and flexible.

However, even if you begin at a prime age, gymnastics may not be your sport. Although the muscles in your arms, legs, and body can be strengthened through proper physical training and you can learn all the gymnastic maneuvers and technique, you must bring a keen sense of balance, a fairly strong yet flexible body, and a good deal of stamina to this very demanding sport. Not everyone can stay balanced while standing on his or her head, walking across a balance beam, or doing a series of somersaults. Gymnastics also requires a high degree of determination, discipline, and hard work, even if you don't strive to be an Olympic star.

If you decide to pursue gymnastics as a recreational activity, you've made a commitment to a relatively inexpensive sport. Gymnastic programs in schools, recreation centers, Y's, and private gymnastic clubs will provide all the necessary equipment and apparatus. All you'll need is a leotard or T-shirt and shorts. Most beginning students perform gymnastic movements barefooted. Later, when you work on the bars, a leather hand grip, which costs $5–$6, may be required.

Your gymnastic session should include at least a 15-minute warm-up, consisting of stretching exercises to loosen the muscles you will use in floor exercises, on the balance beam and other apparatus, and to prevent injury. A series of strengthening exercises such as push-ups and chin-ups to strengthen your arms, sit-ups for strengthening stomach muscles, and reverse sit-ups for strengthening back muscles should also be part of your warm-up program (see the chapter on "Exercising").

Basic gymnastics for both young women and men starts with such tumbling movements as the forward roll, back roll, handstand, cartwheel, roundoff, front and back limber, and handspring. Floor exercises are fundamental to all gymnastic maneuvers. Whatever skills you develop on the floor apply to the apparatus. For example, anything you have learned to do on the floor, you can start to do on the low balance beam. The harder the exercise is on the floor, the harder it will be on the beam. Starting on the low beam, you're likely to learn such movements as the front roll, back roll, and cartwheel, all of which you will later want to master on the high beam.

On the parallel or uneven parallel bars, you'll begin with pullovers (which are similar to chin-

A gymnast does a stag handstand on the floor. (Photo by Ronald Zeiger)

ups), front hip circles (where you roll forward over the bar), and back hip circles (where you flip back over the bar). These movements are similar to the forward and backward rolls done on the floor.

You will also be introduced to some vaulting movements. Vaulting is almost like tumbling except that the exercises are done over a vaulting horse. Because these movements are executed higher off the floor, they require a little more courage on the part of the gymnast. But once you have learned how to run and jump correctly, basic vaulting movements such as the dive roll over the horse, the squat-through, and the handspring will not seem as difficult.

Getting Involved

After your introduction to beginning gymnastics, the best way to get more involved is to join a gymnastic club or enroll in a class at the Y and spend as much time as you can becoming comfortable with the apparatus and perfecting the basics. Once you've mastered them and feel you have a strong foundation in gymnastics, you'll want to practice doing moves in combination instead of separately.

Eventually you may reach a competition level of performance. At this point, you may want to try out for your school gymnastics team or the team of a private club that is sanctioned by the United States Gymnastics Federation. Through your school or club, you will be able to participate in regional, state, and national competitive gymnastic events.

If you aspire to be a serious gymnast or even an Olympic competitor (only fourteen men and women are ultimately chosen to represent each country), then you may want to start looking, while you are in high school, for a college with a strong gymnastics program. Many colleges now offer scholarships to outstanding high school gymnasts.

On the competitive level, women perform prescribed and optional exercises in four events: tumbling, balance beam, uneven parallel bars, and vaulting horse. Men compete in six events: tumbling, side horse, steel rings, vaulting horse, parallel bars, and high bar. In their events, women have an opportunity to display movements requiring considerable grace and flexibility. While grace is equally important in the men's movements, their exercises rely heavily on strength.

Although you may not aim to represent your country in the next Olympics, the hours of warm-up, training, instruction, and performance build self-confidence as well as a strong body, and the personal rewards of small achievements are as important to the recreational gymnast as the gold, silver, and bronze medals are to Olympic competitors.

Inside Tips From the Experts

Ben Corr, assistant coach at a gymnastics center offers these tips to beginning gymnasts:
1. If you are really interested in gymnastics and can afford it, join a private club for the following reasons:
   a. Private clubs provide quality coaching and adequate safety.
   b. A coach at a private club can provide you with proper training supervision, organizing your training towards an effective goal.
   c. The atmosphere at a private club motivates you: in an environment where

everyone is involved in gymnastics, you feel like a gymnast.

2. Gymnastics takes a lot of patience and more heart than talent!

Suggested Reading

Boone, William T. *Better Gymnastics, How to Spot the Performer.* Mountain View, CA: World Publications, 1979.

International Gymnast magazine, Santa Monica, CA: Sundby Publications.

Resnick, Michael. *Gymnastics and You.* New York: Rand McNally and Company, 1977.

ICE SKATING

Getting Started

Ice skating is another example of a sport that just about anybody of any size or age can get started in. It's easy to learn; you need no special physical qualifications or skills. If you have a normal sense of balance, you can learn to skate.

In addition, ice skating is a sport that in one form or another will suit a variety of tastes, interests, and time schedules. With only a few hours a week available, you can skate with your friends at your local rink and have loads of fun without even realizing that you're involved in an excellent form of exercise. If you have visions of being another Dorothy Hamill or Dick Button, United States Olympic gold medal winners in figure skating, or if you simply want to learn some fancy ice maneuvers for the fun of it, you might enroll in a series of figure skating lessons. If you have hopes of being another Eric Heiden, winner of five gold medals in the 1980 Winter Olympic Speed Skating Events, or if you just want to race against other skaters at very fast speeds, you can get started in speed skating. If you'd like a competitive game on ice that requires power skating as well as speed skating, then get involved in ice hockey. If you simply enjoy dancing to music with your favorite partner, you may decide to take up ice dancing.

No matter what form of ice skating you'd like to take up, your enjoyment and skills will be improved by taking lessons. Lessons grouped by age and ability are usually offered at your local ice skating rink. An excellent national group lesson program is sponsored by the Ice Skating Institute of America. Professional figure skating teachers take you through five learning stages: Pre-Alpha, learning how to stay balanced on skates; Alpha, learning how to skate and stop in a forward direction; Beta, learning how to skate and stop in a backward direction; Gamma, learning how to turn from front to back; and Delta, learning more advanced techniques. This series of lessons is excellent for learning skating basics, even if you're not specifically interested in figure skating.

When first beginning, it's highly recommended that you rent your skates from your local ice skating rink until you're absolutely sure you want to pursue ice skating. Be sure to lace your skates tightly in the area around the ankles where you'll need the most support. The laces should be slightly looser at the very top so as not to cut off circulation to the foot. Remember to dress warmly, according to the weather. If the weather is cold and rainy, it's going to be even colder and damper at the rink. Wear regular warm clothing, including long pants or jeans, and don't forget a pair of gloves or mittens.

Nothing improves your skating more than practicing what you've learned in your lessons. The prices of your lesson usually includes some practice time. Of course, the first time on skates you're going to feel a little unsteady. It's recommended that you use the guide rail around the rink to steady yourself while you're getting the feel of your blades. Before trying to skate, stand still with your feet parallel, your weight balanced on both skates and one hand on the rail. Next stand sideways, one hand still holding on to the rail, and try sliding your blades back and forth. When you feel steady enough, try pushing off with your left skate, bringing your skates together, gliding, then pushing with the right, and so forth. Take short steps, keeping your ankles as straight as you can. If necessary, continue gripping the rail, but let go of it just as soon as you have found your balance. Once you get the hang of moving on skates, you will

A forward crossover. (Courtesy of Mano Foto)

Skating backwards. (Courtesy of Mano Foto)

progress to taking longer strokes, making various stops, skating backwards, skating on your edges, and doing crossovers, turns, spins, spirals, jumps, and other exciting moves that you will be introduced to in your lessons. You must master the basics of skating before you try speed skating, power skating (ice hockey), or any other kind of skating.

In speed skating, you can race for fun in informal races of any distance with your friends, or you can compete in indoor and outdoor mass events over specific distances measured in meters. In these events all the skaters start at the same time and the winner is the first skater to cross the finish line. Olympic-style events are races where speed skaters race against the clock. The winner is the skater who finishes a measured distance first.

For effective speed skating—no matter what type of race you're in—you'll have to learn the proper starting stance, the body position for racing, the placement of the feet on the ice, various strides for straightaway and for turns, and skating strategy. In addition, to be in top shape for speed skating, your legs have to be strong and you need a lot of stamina. A year-round exercise program—including cycling, running, walking, calisthenics, and any other exercises specifically tailored to increase your wind capacity and the strength in your legs — is essential to speed skating (see chapter on "Exercising").

To get started in ice hockey you'll need to learn the basic skating techniques, and in addition, how to skate forward and backward at fast speeds; how to change direction quickly (which some experts believe is the most important part of the game); how to handle a hockey stick; how to skate with a puck; how to pass, shoot, intercept; and how to play the game both offensively and defensively.

The best way to learn these fundamentals is through a beginner's hockey program, usually offered by a hockey club at a local ice skating rink. Besides teaching you fundamentals, this type of program gives you a chance to see if you like ice hockey and want to continue playing before buying any equipment. Most beginner's programs will lend you a helmet and a hockey stick. In some areas of the country where interest in junior ice hockey runs high, you may be loaned or even given all the equipment. In either case, all you'll need to do is rent a pair of hockey skates.

The more time you spend on the ice, the better you'll play hockey. Off the ice you can practice hockey basics by playing street hockey. In this game, you'll have a chance to practice stick handling and shooting. In a short while, you'll be able to join a house league where you play local teams or, if you're good enough, a traveling team which competes against other teams in your area of the country.

Many young people suffering from asthma, hay fever, and other allergies, who cannot exercise outdoors, really appreciate the nonallergenic, cold environment of the ice rink. Other teenagers simply like activities on the ice because they offer an exciting and challenging way to exercise and have fun.

Equipment

Since all you really need to start is a pair of skates, recreational ice skating is a fairly inexpensive sport. Unless you're a serious skater, you don't need to buy new skates. For quite a while, you can rent them from the rink for a minimal charge of about $1–$2 per session. You may even know someone who has a pair of skates that he or she has outgrown or doesn't use and is willing to pass on to you. Used skates are often sold at garage sales, flea markets, and skate shops at the ice rink. If the skates are the right size for you, you can usually purchase them at a reasonable price, have them sharpened at the skate shop for a small fee, and thus own an inexpensive, usable pair of skates. Sometimes used skates are also sold through newspaper ads (under sporting equipment) or on bulletin boards at the ice skating rink.

If you plan to do more than recreational skating and plan to skate often, you may want to purchase new skates. Quality figure skates made of leather with steel blades cost anywhere from about $83–$220. Cheaper skates made with plastic and vinyl boots can be bought, but it pays to buy the best skates you can afford. Ice skates with the boot custom-made for your foot and quality blades purchased separately can cost as much as $330. No matter what ice skates you choose, the best place to be fitted for them is the skate shop at the ice rink. To protect your blades when you're off the ice, it's a good idea to spend a couple of dollars for a pair of skate guards.

Figure skating accessories for young women include skating dresses, which cost anywhere from about $20–$55, and tights, which cost around $6. A complete warm-up suit, consisting of a tight-fitting nylon jacket and pants, costs anywhere from $83–$94 and is often worn by men as well as women.

American-made speed skates of lightweight but tough kangaroo leather with thin steel blades cost around $77. European, custom-made speed skates can cost as much as $165.

Except on the highly competitive level, regular tight-fitting clothing is usually worn by speed skaters.

Most hockey skates are made of vinyl with plastic supports sewn in, plastic bottoms, and a lightweight steel blade. Hockey skates cost anywhere from $28–$187. When you purchase a better hockey skate, the blades are usually sold separately from the boot. Superior hockey blades are made of stainless steel. When buying new hockey skates, it's wise to purchase them at the rink skate shop. Experienced personnel will know what type of hockey skate is best for your age, size, level of play, and playing position. If you plan to buy new skates, get them in September — at the beginning of the hockey season — so that you can get maximum use from your skates before outgrowing them. To keep your skates in top playing condition, you'll need to get them sharpened at least twice a month.

Since ice hockey is a body contact sport much like football, protective equipment must be worn on the ice. Used hockey skates and the necessary protective equipment can often be purchased from other players or at club swaps. Team jerseys are usually provided by the club. If you must purchase new protective equipment, which includes elbow, leg, and shin guards, athletic support, protective pants, shoulder pads, helmet and face mask, gloves, socks, and suspenders, your initial outlay will be anywhere from $138–$165. However, when you've outgrown it, you'll probably be able to sell much of this equipment to another member of your club.

Getting Involved

Once you have your equipment and have mastered the basics, many more challenging ice activities await you. Perhaps at this point you'll be interested in taking private lessons or joining a skating club.

Ice dancing (ballroom dancing on ice) has recently become an event in the Winter Olympics. Through a skating club, you can compete in nonqualifying competitions on the regional level. In these less competitive events, you and your partner of the opposite sex must perform both established dance patterns and original routines on ice and to music. Your skating club or local rink will be able to tell you when and where these regional competitions take place.

The Amateur Hockey Association of the United States organizes regional, amateur ice hockey for young people from five to nineteen. Teams within a club are divided by age: Mites, 5 to 8; Squirts, 9 to 10; Peewees, 11 to 12; Bantams, 13 to 14; Midgets, 15 to 16; and Juniors, 17 to 19. Teams usually have at least one practice session and one game a week during the season, and they compete against other local or regional teams of equal age and ability. Winners of a region in each age group compete against one another in state tournaments. The best players of each team in each age division are selected to make up a regional AAA All-Star Ice Hockey team. These teams compete against each other in regional play-offs. The winners move on to state and national competitions.

If you become an outstanding ice hockey player of all-star caliber, you may be interested in enrolling in an Eastern college preparatory school that has a hockey team. Some American and Canadian professional ice hockey teams recruit exceptional players, ages fifteen and up, for their farm teams. From high school ice hockey teams or farm teams, the next step may be playing professional ice hockey in the National Hockey League.

Inside Tips From the Experts

Evelynne Gill, a professional figure skating teacher, suggests the following to beginning skaters:

1. Lessons, group or private, will help you enjoy figure skating much more. Expert tips can make executing that turn so much easier.
2. The more you skate, the faster you learn. Practice two or three times a week.
3. If you're not falling, you're not learning.
4. Push yourself a little bit further than you think you can go.
5. The best place to buy equipment is at the rink, where you can buy good skates, get a good fit, and have your skates sharpened.

Suggested Reading

Dolan, Edward F., Jr. *The Complete Beginner's Guide to Ice Skating.* New York: Doubleday and Co., Garden City, 1974.

Skating magazine, U.S. Figure Skating Assn., Boston, MA.

USFSA's Program Aids Series: Guides to Skating Activities. *Basic Tests, Beginner's Hockey, Precision Skating* (Available free of charge upon request from the U.S. Figure Skating Assn.).

JOGGING

Getting Started

Before you take your first steps out the door and on the jogging path or running track, take some time to evaluate your fitness. If you're in your teens, you're probably in pretty good shape and can engage in any form of physical exercise. But just to be on the safe side, it's best to have had a medical checkup within the past year showing that you're in good health before beginning any jogging activity. If you're very overweight, you're subject to extra jarring of your joints, and possible injury. It's wise to lose some weight and engage in such sports as swimming and walking before taking up jogging. In addition, if you suffer from any foot or leg disorders, such as Morton's foot (where your second toe is longer than your big toe), Cavus foot (high arch), flat foot (no arch), knock-knees, bowlegs, bunions, or corns, you may be more prone to running injuries. If, as a result of any of these conditions, you experience pain while jogging, see a sports podiatrist for recommendations regarding special running shoes and running techniques to help you overcome your condition. In years past, people with these problems would very likely have been advised to stop running.

Once you've determined you're in good enough shape to run, use the following jogging program—or one like it—as your daily guide and stick to it as closely as you can.

THE WORKOUT

Step 1. Set aside about an hour, any time during the day, for this workout. There's no best time to jog and you can vary the time each day. Change into your jogging clothes and get ready for this new activity by relaxing for one to two minutes. Close your eyes. Clear your mind. Take a deep breath. Completely relax your muscles. Consciously separate this activity from whatever you were doing before.

Step 2. Before you can do any warm-up stretching exercises (Step 3), you need to get your heart rate and body temperature up. This can be done by jogging in place and doing jumping jacks for one to five minutes, or until you are about to break into a sweat.

Step 3. *The Golden Five Stretches for Joggers*
Stretching is the most important part of any jogging program. Stretching *before* you jog prepares you for running by loosening your muscles, and it also helps you avoid pulling and straining your muscles and tendons. Stretching *after* you jog offsets the shortening or contracting of the muscles that occurs when you jog.

As you do each of the recommended stretching exercises, you'll feel a pleasant burning sensation, and you may even feel the muscles stretch. Hold the stretch about 30 seconds and then slack off. Do not stretch to the point of pain, and *do not bounce*. Repeat the stretch one or two times. Stretching properly is vitally important. Don't cut corners by leaving out this step in your workout.

Hamstring Stretch Lift your leg onto a chair or bar so that it is at a 90° angle to your other leg. Keep your back straight and stretch out the raised leg for about 30 seconds. Alternate legs.

Hamstring stretch. (Photo by Ronald Zeiger)

Calf Stretch Stand about 3 feet away from a wall or tree. Place your palms against one of these surfaces and with your feet together—heels flat, knees locked, and back straight—push against the wall or tree.

Calf stretch. (Photo by Ronald Zeiger)

Achilles Stretch Put your weight on your front foot and keep your rear heel planted. Bend your front knee and push it down toward the ground as far as it will go. This stretches the rear leg.

Achilles stretch. (Photo by Ronald Zeiger)

Quadriceps Stretch Balancing on your right leg, bend the other knee, lifting the left foot back and up until you can grab it at the ankle. Gently pull the leg upward while leaning slightly forward. Hold for 30 seconds. Then alternate legs.

Groin Stretch In a sitting position, place the soles of your feet together. Hold your ankles and press down on your knees with your elbows. When beginning, be careful not to overdo this stretch.

Quadriceps stretch and groin stretch. (Photo by Ronald Zeiger)

Step 4. Jog for 20 minutes at least 3 times a week at your best comfortable pace. On these days—your hard workout days—you can jog, walk, sprint, or vary the pace, but don't be concerned about speed or distance. You don't have to jog the whole time. If it becomes hard for you to breathe, slack off to a slow jog or walk until you catch your breath. Then jog or run again. Remember, it's the time, not the speed or distance,

that counts. On the days you're not jogging—
your easy days—put on your jogging clothes,
stretch, take a walk or a bike ride, or spend the
time at some other sport. Just get in the habit
of setting aside this time for some kind of workout. Your weekly workout schedule should include at least three hard days, three easy days,
and one day of rest.

Step 5. Complete your run by winding down
to a slow jog or walk. Then repeat all the stretching exercises in Step 2. Cool down a few minutes before taking a moderate shower, not too
hot or too cold.

After your workout, you should feel as if
you've exerted yourself, but you should not feel
exhausted. If you do feel exhausted, then you
have jogged too far and/or too fast. After a month
or two of following this program, you should
be able to gradually increase your speed or distance. When you do, remember the most important rule for the beginning jogger: "Train,
don't strain."

Equipment

A pair of running shoes is the single most
important jogging accessory. You can run in just
about any kind of clothing—gym shorts or cut-
off jeans and a T-shirt, a sweat suit, even a bath-
ing suit; but don't shortchange yourself when
purchasing the shoes. Buy running shoes from
a company that specializes in manufacturing
them. A good pair will cost anywhere from
$22–$50. Adidas, Puma, Nike, Brooks, and New
Balance are brand names of excellent running

shoes. Look for lightweight nylon and leather shoes that fit tightly in the heel and have plenty of room in the toe.

Your shorts and shirt should be loose-fitting, comfortable, and not cause any irritation. Shorts made of nylon tricot are light in weight and cause little or no chafing. They are often worn by runners for these reasons.

Women should wear a jogging bra when running. Look for the one-size-fits-all kind that is made of stretchy material and has few seams and no metal buckles or fasteners. Men should wear jockey shorts or an athletic supporter under their running shorts.

A single pair of clean cotton, orlon, or wool socks should be worn by all joggers.

Getting Involved

One of the delights of jogging is that you're free to jog anywhere. Without equipment to carry or a bus to catch, you can run out the front door and around the block. You can jog in a park, on your local school track, or on country roads and mountain trails. All the outdoors is your running course.

In addition to being able to jog over varying terrains, you can jog at different speeds. The Swedes call this type of running *fartlek*, or speed play. Try running on forest trails, through flat meadows, and up hills, at different paces, playing as you run. Run backwards and sideways, do crossovers, sprint, take long and leaping strides, run in a zigzag pattern, or jump over obstacles such as logs and hedges. Then jog at your normal pace for 400 yards. This type of running is especially recommended for soccer and football players and other people who want to condition themselves for a particular sport.

LSD, or long slow distance, is another method of running recommended for the beginning jogger. In LSD running, you jog at 60 percent of your normal maximum speed, keeping a slow, steady, untimed pace. If you jog at this leisurely pace, you're apt to enjoy your run more and feel fewer aches and pains afterward. In addition, LSD running will increase your endurance, distance, and—in time—your speed. If you're a little overweight, a long, slow run for at least 40 minutes once a week will help turn your body into a more efficient fat burner, and you'll soon discover you're losing weight.

For building stamina, try resistance running. Run up hills, through knee-deep water, or through sand.

For an opportunity to be with your family, run with your parents and sisters and brothers. Jogging is one of the few activities families can do together.

If you can't resist the competitive urge to run in a race, start by entering a fun-run in your area. These races are usually held on weekends and are sponsored by a fund-raising or cultural group, a running club, or a city. Participants enter the race by age classification: usually 14 and under, and 15 to 29. Once you have entered one race, you will be given information about other races.

Family runs, where mothers run with daughters or fathers with sons, are often sponsored by running clubs. Relay races and dual races, where running is combined with another activity such as swimming, are exciting races to enter. Sport stores that specialize in selling running shoes usually announce all kinds of running events on their bulletin boards. By joining a club, you can keep in touch with what's happening in the running world in your community and elsewhere.

Running is one sport where you don't have to be competitive. Run, but run for fun!

Inside Tips From the Experts

Robert E. Burger, author of *Jogger's Catalog* and an avid runner, offers these tips to beginning joggers and runners:

1. Don't jog on concrete and cement exclusively. You're more likely to jog injury-free on dirt or grass.
2. A healthy athlete can be hurt by heat. Don't run in the heat of the day. Drink plenty of water in warm weather—temperatures of 75° and up. During warm spells, slow down your pace by a minute per mile.
3. Don't be surprised if you have aches and pains at first. They are part of muscle development. However, don't ignore unusual pains that are persistent. If you injure yourself don't run until your injury is healed. Swim or do some other aerobic sport at a level that doesn't aggravate your injury.
4. Don't time yourself or try to measure your distance. The increase in distance will come naturally.
5. It's better to own two medium-priced pairs

of running shoes than one very expensive pair. Your feet will feel more comfortable when you alternate wearing two pairs.

Suggested Reading

Burger, Robert E. *Jogger's Catalog*. New York: M. Evans and Co., 1978.

Fixx, James F. *The Complete Book of Running*. New York: Random House, 1977.

Runner's World magazine, Mountain View, CA.

JUGGLING

Getting Started

If you're age ten or older, have an average amount of coordination, and can throw and catch a ball—or even if you're a total "klutz"!—you can learn to juggle. You don't need to purchase any expensive equipment. You can learn to juggle with three of many of the things you have around the house—pieces of fruit, soda cans, even hard-boiled eggs. (When you get really good at juggling, you won't have to boil them!)

To slow down the action while you're learning, you can tie a knot in the ends of some silk or nylon scarves and juggle them. At first you may find juggling easier if you use objects that don't roll. You'll spend more time chasing after rubber balls than trying to juggle them.

A friend, a juggling teacher, or a beginner's book on juggling can introduce you to the three basic patterns: the Cascade, the One-Handed, and the Shower. In the Cascade pattern, three objects cross back and forth between the hands; in the One-Handed, two or more objects are tossed side by side or in circles in one hand; in the Shower, all the objects are tossed with one hand and caught with the other. The next time you see a sidewalk juggler or someone juggling

Remember, juggling is the art of keeping one object (not three!) in the air. (UPI)

in the park, watch for these patterns.

Other juggling patterns are based on the Cascade. To do the Cascade you hold two objects in one hand and one in the other. Starting with your two-object hand, say your right hand, toss one of the objects in an arc over toward your left hand. While this object is arching its way over, you'll still be holding one object in each hand. As the first object begins to drop down toward your left hand, pop the second object out of that hand (the left), tossing it just to the inside of the dropping object's arc. The two objects should pass one another about six inches above your left hand. (This step is called an exchange.) As the second object drops toward your right hand, exchange it for the third object, which then begins *its* journey over to your left hand. As soon as you can do two exchanges in a row, take a break and a bow. You're juggling!

Practice juggling in front of a wall so that you can't throw your objects too far out in front of you. Keep your tosses all on the same plane as if the objects were being tossed in a picture frame. Most important, remember that juggling is the art of keeping one object in the air, not three!

The First Exchange in the Cascade

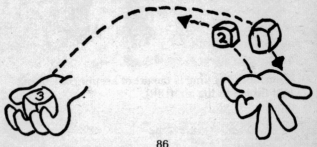

Equipment

Once you've successfully juggled with just about everything you can find around the house, you may want to try balls and some of the other objects preferred by professional jugglers. An inexpensive way to do this is to fill the two halves of a tennis ball with sand and then tape them back together to form one weighted ball. The ball should weigh from 4 to 6 ounces. Canadian lacrosse balls are also excellent for juggling. They are sold in large sporting goods stores and cost $2–$3 each. Solid rubber balls, the kind sold in pet shops, also work well.

Eventually you may want to feel even more like a professional and use clubs. You can make your own set from one quart plastic bleach bottles and pieces of mop handles or broomsticks. The following diagram shows you how.

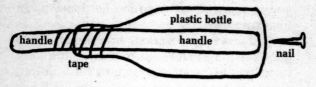

Ken Benge, in *The Art of Juggling* (see "Suggested Reading"), describes some excellent methods for making juggling rings. Once you have decided on the size you want, cut them out from either a piece of wood veneer or a piece of plastic recommended for juggling rings. Smooth the edges by sanding them. Wrap the wooden rings with plastic tape to make them last longer. For a finishing touch, you can decorate your rings with geometric designs and other attractive patterns.

Once you can juggle with standard size balls, clubs, and rings, you can also learn to juggle with variations of these basic shapes. When you're good enough, try juggling with basketballs, walnuts, tennis rackets, canes, hula hoops, and bicycle rims. There's no limit to the things you can juggle!

Getting Involved

Once you've learned the basic patterns of juggling three objects, you will want to learn how to keep four and five objects going and other fancy tricks. You might want to try team juggling with a partner. Together you can work on such maneuvers as stealing (where you interrupt your partner's juggling and steal two objects), and passing (where you face your partner and toss objects to his or her left hand rather than your own).

It's fun to try juggling with fruits. Using grapes, you can end your routine by throwing them high in the air and catching them in your mouth. Using three apples, one green and two red, you can do the Eat-the-Apple Trick, where you take a bite out of the green apple, eating it all in stages as you juggle. Other flashy tricks include tossing an object behind your back or under your leg, or catching your final tossed object under your neck. Instruction from an accomplished juggler or a good book on juggling (see "Suggested Reading") and practice are the best ways to master the more difficult tricks.

Inside Tips From the Experts

John Cassidy, author of *Juggling For The Complete Klutz*, and Bill Barr, professional juggler, make these suggestions for anyone who is learning to juggle:

1. Practice the first exchange over and over again until you can do it with fairly frequent consistency. Then move on to the second exchange.
2. Practice with exaggerated slowness and concentrate mainly on your tosses. The catches are secondary. They'll come along by themselves when your throws get ironed out.
3. If your legs are killing you from picking up your drops all the time, stand over a table or a bed.
4. Take frequent breaks while you're trying to learn. Twenty minutes spent in two ten-minute spurts is much more effective than in one lump.
5. If your tosses begin to fly away from you, don't panic. This happens to everyone. Just remember to keep your exchanges in one plane by tossing each object to the inside of the dropping object's arc.
6. As soon as you can, find a competent juggler and have that person show you how to do the Cascade.

Suggested Reading

Benge, Ken. *The Art of Juggling*. Mountain View, CA: World Publications, 1977.

Cassidy, John. *Juggling For The Complete Klutz*. Stanford, CA: Klutz Enterprises, 1977.

MARTIAL ARTS

Among the most popular of the martial arts today are karate, tae kwon do, kung fu, judo, and aikido. Each is an ancient, oriental system of self-defense, artistic expression, physical exercise, and mental discipline. Although similar in these ways, they differ in how they are taught and how the mind and body are trained.

Karate, meaning "empty hands," is the Japanese art of self-defense which, like all martial arts, stresses spiritual as well as physical development. In karate, every muscle is under tension at the end of a punching, kicking, striking, or blocking technique. Because of the tensing of the muscles, karate is considered a hard style of self-defense.

Tae kwon do is the Korean hard style of karate. Translated literally tae kwon do means "the way of kicking and punching." This system places more emphasis on leg techniques than on the hand movements associated with Japanese karate. Tae kwon do also relies on speed, rhythm, and specified stances in all of its offensive and defensive patterns. Experts in this martial art often demonstrate their strength, power, and control by breaking boards and bricks.

Kung fu is the old Chinese style of karate. There are hundreds of different styles, some relying on power and strength techniques, others involving slow, flowing movements and continuous, circular motions.

Judo is an outgrowth of the fighting methods of feudal Japan. Literally, the word means "the way of yielding," "giving way," or "the gentle way." To throw an opponent down, judo employs such techniques as stepping out of the way to throw the attacker off balance, using the opponent's weight and effort to defeat him. Since the opponent's own force aids you in winning, success does not depend on physical size or strength. Agility and timing bring about success in judo.

Aikido, another Japanese art, is primarily defensive, relying on the principles of yielding and waiting peacefully until attacked. These defensive techniques stress not causing any unnecessary pain to the attacker. Aikido, the gentlest of the martial arts, is often referred to as the art of doing nothing.

Getting Started

You don't have to be a certain age, sex, or size to get started in one of the martial arts. There's a system of self-defense to suit almost every body type and personality.

Most martial arts classes are taught in private studios by private instructors. Sometimes a local Parks and Recreation Department will sponsor a program in a community center. Local Y's often offer classes in judo. Private studios and schools are listed in the yellow pages of the phone book, but the best way to find a good class and instructor is by word of mouth. No matter how you find out about a particular school, check out its reputation before enrolling. Here's what to look for in choosing a reputable school:

1. Make sure the instructor will let you watch a class before you start taking lessons. Otherwise, don't enroll.
2. Observe a class to see if the method of instruction suits you.
3. Check to see if the atmosphere of the school makes you feel comfortable. Don't get bullied into joining a school or paying money if you feel the place isn't right for you.
4. Most likely you, your parents, or another adult will have to sign a waiver stating that the school or instructor is not liable if you injure yourself during a lesson.
5. Look for a school where you pay month to month.
6. Beware of schools where you must sign a contract stating your payments must continue over a certain period of time whether or not you want to continue your lessons.
7. Look for a school as close to your home as possible.

Most martial arts programs start you off with a warm-up period consisting of stretching exercises and calisthenics. Part of your class time may be devoted to learning and practicing basic techniques such as kicking, punching, and blocking. In another segment of the lesson you may engage in an imaginary fight. Your instructor may require you to go through a prearranged set of motions as if you were encountering a real opponent. In some classes you may do free sparring where you use the basic moves, improvise, and practice what you have learned by play fighting. In some styles you'll actually make contact with your opponent; in others you'll stop about an inch before contact, testing your concentration and control.

Equipment

The equipment you'll need to get started in any of the martial arts is inexpensive and simple. For karate and tae kwon do, you'll need an outfit called a gi, which consists of a pair of cotton or cotton polyester pants and a loose-fitting jacket that allows lots of room for movement of the arms and body. To start, a white belt is also required. When beginning, buy a less expensive gi unless you're absolutely sure you're serious enough from the start to want to continue over a long period. Inexpensive gis cost anywhere from about $22–$33, but you can pay up to $83 or more for a better-quality outfit. Women usually wear a T-shirt under their gi.

For judo and aikido, you'll wear an outfit, also called a gi, consisting of a padded jacket and pants with padding at the knees. Gis for judo and aikido are made of very heavy cotton. The outfit has to be durable enough to withstand pulling and throwing. A white belt, which is wrapped around the waist twice, is also worn. In the inexpensive range, these outfits cost from $22–$33. More expensive gis, not recommended for beginners, cost anywhere from about $83–$110.

Advanced aikido students may be required

to wear hakimas, which are very full pleated pants. Because of the many pleats in these garments, those made of permanent press material are recommended over the cotton ones, which require ironing.

This young martial arts expert has earned a purple belt in karate, the Japanese sport of self-defense. (Ken Levinson)

For kung fu, lightweight polyester or cotton pants and a T-shirt are worn. Some students of kung fu also wear a pair of lightweight, black cotton shoes, which cost about $6.

Getting Involved

After three or four months of training in the basic techniques, you'll probably be ready to take your first promotion test. You'll be asked to demonstrate what you have learned in your lessons. Each school has its own system of colored belts to show your rank. After your first promotion test, you'll continue to refine your basic techniques, learn more advanced moves, take more promotion tests, and move up in rank.

Eventually you may want to compete in martial arts tournaments. Often an instructor of a particular school will sponsor a local tournament and students from various schools in the area will participate. Check your area to see what is available.

Inside Tips From the Experts

Stefan Argent and Alan Bultoch, both students of the martial arts and salesmen of martial arts equipment, offer these inside tips:

1. Look for a school that doesn't expose you to any risk until you're ready for it.
2. Since martial arts styles vary from no contact to full or heavy contact, choose a style that suits your emotional makeup and physical ability.
3. Included with physical training in the martial arts is training in the Oriental Buddhist

tradition. Physical and spiritual training go hand in hand for a full appreciation of the Oriental martial arts.

4. If the instructor does not include the spiritual as well as the physical training, be wary of the school.

Suggested Reading

Black Belt magazine, Rainbow Publications, Burbank, CA.

Karate Illustrated magazine, Rainbow Publications, Burbank, CA.

Kozuki, Russell. *Karate For Young People*. New York: Cornerstone Library, 1975.

Ribner, Susan, and Chin, Richard, Dr. *The Martial Arts*. New York: Harper and Row Publishers, 1978.

MOTORCYCLING

Getting Started

In most states, if you are under a certain age, usually sixteen, the law forbids you to ride your cycle anywhere except off the road. If you're not "street legal," you'll have to walk your cycle to an off-road area where you can ride it. Once you get off the road, there may still be restrictions. Throughout the country, laws make off-road riding on private property without the owner's permission a crime for motorcyclists. You must confine your riding to approved open land, dirt roads, trails, motorcycle parks—areas specially designated for off-road riding, *places where you are absolutely sure motorcycling is permitted*. In addition, most off-road cycles, unless they have certain modifications for street riding, are illegal on the road.

Although you may not be old enough to obtain a special motorcycle license to ride on the street, most states do require that you register your motorcycle. In addition, *in some states it is illegal to ride your motorcycle without a helmet, eye protection, or a crash bar*. Since the laws governing motorcycle riding vary from state to state and even from year to year, it is your responsibility to check with your local Department of Motor Vehicles, Highway Patrol, or other law enforcement agency to *acquaint yourself with every law pertaining to your cycle and where and how you may ride it.* Ignorance of the law is no excuse for motorcyclists.

Once you know the motorcycle laws of your state, someone will have to teach you how to ride: the proper way to get on your motorcycle, start it, feel balanced on it, shift gears, work all the controls, accelerate, coast, slow down, stop, dismount, and park.

If you're buying a new motorcycle, make sure someone in the sales or service department at the motorcycle dealership is willing to show you how to operate your motorcycle. Buy your cycle only from a dealer who will go through the basic operation of your machine with you. With the purchase of a new bike, you'll receive an owner's instruction manual, which you should read from cover to cover.

Even though a reputable dealer shows you how to operate the controls on your new motorcycle and you read every word of your owner's manual, these preliminary introductions to motorcycle riding should not take the place of qualified instruction in a formal, off-road motorcycle riding training program. To learn how to ride safely and properly, you must participate in an off-road youth riding program. Your motorcycle dealer may know of one. Or check with your local Y or 4-H Club to see if they offer any kind of instruction. In some high schools, learning to ride a motorcycle is part of the driver education training program.

Equipment

Buying a motorcycle by brand name alone is not the best way to make this expensive purchase. A better way to go about purchasing a new motorcycle is to talk to motorcycle owners and to several different motorcycle dealers in your area. Other riders are likely to know what kind of riding is available near you and what cycles are best suited for that type of terrain. By talking to several motorcycle dealers, you'll find out which dealership is most willing to help you select your bike, learn how to ride it, and service it. Once you've talked with other riders and discovered a dealership that cares about your first motorcycle purchase, don't stop there. Do some thinking about your own capabilities, limitations, and preferences. Take into consideration your physical size, strength, and coordination; and also think seriously about how you plan to use your cycle. Now you're ready to select and purchase a motorcycle.

At this point, you're probably interested in purchasing a competition bike, mini-bike, playbike, trail bike, or dual-purpose machine—a two-wheeled vehicle that's built for off-the-road travel.

Even when you eliminate all the street motorcycles, the numbers of choices in off-road models can overwhelm the first-time buyer. One manufacturer alone produces about twenty-five different models of off-road motorcycles.

Fortunately, the selection narrows somewhat when you realize you'll be choosing from models that are built for your size and strength. Take special care that your new bike is not too heavy or powerful for you—too much machine for you to handle. For off-road riding, the lighter and more maneuverable the bike, the easier it will be for you to control it on rough terrain, through sand and dirt, and over rocks, stumps, and hills.

If you've done your homework, you'll know by the time you arrive at the motorcycle dealership whether you want a mini or playbike for off-road fun and playing in the dirt; a motocross for racing on short, rough, and severely humped

Off-road cycles feature plastic and aluminum parts, knobby-style tires, and suspension systems with longer travel. (Photo by Ronald Zeiger)

track; an enduro bike for endurance competition on nearly impassable terrain; a trail bike for "cow-trailing" and getting off into the woods; or a dual-purpose bike that's street legal but can be ridden on dirt as well.

Most of these dirt bikes feature plastic and aluminum alloy parts that are strong but light, knobby-style tires for better traction, and modern suspension systems for riding on rough terrain. As for engine size, most motorcycle dealers recommend that first-time riders start out on bikes ranging from 50 to 80 cubic centimeters for youngsters six to twelve years of age, 80 to 125 cubic centimeters for young people from twelve to fifteen, and 125 to 250 cubic centimeters for fifteen- and sixteen-year-olds. Of course, your own size, strength, weight, and ability will ultimately determine what motorcycle "fits" you best. Reputable dealers will encourage you to climb aboard the motorcycle of your choice. When seated, you should be able to get both feet down flat on the floor. If you can't, you should choose a smaller model.

Buying a new motorcycle is no small purchase, so be absolutely sure you've chosen the bike that's right for you. Off-the-road motorcycles with engine sizes of 50 to 80 cubic centimeters cost anywhere from $550–$880; 80 to 125 cubic centimeters, from $880–$1,430; 125 to 250 cubic centimeters, $1,100–$1,650.

These prices may make buying a new bike impossible for you, so think about buying a used one instead. If you've located a used cycle you think you'd like to own, don't buy it until you've had it checked out by an experienced motorcycle mechanic. For a small fee service departments at motorcycle dealerships will gladly test-ride and inspect a used bike of their own brand. A mechanic will tell you honestly whether the bike you're looking at is a lemon or a good buy. If he tells you not to spend your money on it, take his advice. Remember, you're looking for a used bike, not an abused bike!

Whether or not your state requires that you wear a helmet and goggles when motorcycle riding, it is foolish to do any type of cycling without them. Approved fiberglass helmets cost anywhere from about $28—$143. Buy the very best you can afford. It's worth it. Plastic goggles cost about $6–$22. Leather or leather-and-nylon gloves, ranging in price from $6–33, are worn for hand protection and to get a better grip. To protect your legs and arms, long pants and long sleeves are worn by motorcyclists—the heavier the material, the better. Although you can buy sophisticated, plastic riding boots that cost as much as $220, a sturdy pair of leather work boots or hiking boots will do just as well. High-topped, lace-up boots, rather than loose ones, are recommended for several reasons. They give your ankles more support, keep them from bending, and in case your leg or foot is injured in an accident, can be taken off easier. If you plan to get involved in racing, you may want to purchase a nylon-and-cotton racing jersey, which costs from $17–$33, and leather or nylon-and-leather racing pants, which cost from $33–$187. For racing, a chest protector, which costs about $44, is also worn.

A helmet, goggles, long-sleeved shirt, long pants, gloves, and work boots fully protect this off-road rider. (Photo by Ronald Zeiger)

Getting Involved

Once you feel confident about handling your new motorcycle and have had some riding experience, you'll be looking for new challenges. For starters, try riding river bottoms, climbing hills, riding on desert terrain, or cow-trailing. Wherever you cycle, it's safer and more fun to go with friends. *If you do go riding alone, make sure you've told someone where you are going and what time to expect you back. Always wear your helmet and goggles.*

To get involved in organized motorcycling events, you may want to join a junior motorcycle club. Your motorcycle dealer should be able to help you find a club in your locality. In addition, dealers often post notices about races and other motorcycle activities on bulletin boards in their showrooms. Motorcycle magazines and newspapers such as *Cycle News* also carry announcements of motorcycle races.

The most popular type of racing among teenagers today is motocross. In motocross you race on a track anywhere from one-half mile to two miles long through water and mud hazards, over jumps, around tricky corners, and up and down hills. But motocross races are not held in every region of the country. Scrambles, hill climbs, enduro, and flat and short track races are other types of races in which you may want to participate. A scramble is a race over a closed course a half-mile to two miles in length on a graded track. Often a jump is included. In hill climbing races, the object is to race against the clock up a steep hill. Flat track races are held on dirt ovals of a quarter-mile to a mile in length, while short track races are always a quarter-mile long. Enduros, so named because they require great tests of endurance rather than speed, are non-speed events over varying terrain. Riders must maintain a certain average speed while traveling distances ranging from 20 to 400 miles.

No matter what type of racing you plan to get involved in, you'll be off to a better start if you watch several races before entering one yourself. Before you actually race, find out what release and entry forms, special licenses, and fees are required. Ask other racers what protective clothing is recommended and what you should do to get in shape for racing. Motocross racing is considered the second most demanding sport; only soccer is more rigorous. When you're finally ready for your first race, enter it in the lowest class, usually called the novice class or "C" class.

With the wind whistling past you, it's quite a thrill to maneuver your off-road cycle down a back road or around a dirt track at top speeds. But no matter how good you become at handling your off-road cycle, *always remember that these off-road skills do not qualify you to be a safe rider on the street.*

Inside Tips From the Experts

Trisha Yeager, author of a motorcycle manual for women, hopes teenagers will keep the following motorcycling safety tips in mind at all times when riding:

1. *Learn to ride a motorcycle the safe way.* Take an approved motorcycle rider course. Such courses may be offered in high schools, by public service organizations, or by the highway patrol. They teach the dynamics of motorcycles, safe operating techniques, and how to react in simulated emergency situations. To find out the availability of a rider education course in your area, ask your motorcycle dealer or write to the Motorcycle Safety Foundation.

2. *Be aware that you are vulnerable to accidents, and use this awareness to be as safe as possible.* A recent study of motorcycle accidents, injuries, and fatalities has determined that teenage riders are involved in more than half of all the accidents studied. Rider training and education, while not the whole answer, is a big step forward in the reduction of accidents.

3. *Never ride a motorcycle while under the influence of drugs, alcohol, or medication that might alter your awareness, perceptions, or reflexes.* Fatigue, too, can slow down your reflexes and alter your perceptions and responses.

4. *Always drive defensively.* Anticipate what other drivers might do, and keep a cushion of space around yourself at all times. Remember, you simply don't have the protection on a motorcycle that you do in a car.

5. *Always wear a helmet and other protective attire while riding.*

6. *Make yourself as visible as possible.* Wear bright colors like yellow and orange while riding.

7. *Resist the temptation to feel overly confident.* Beginning motorcyclists sometimes think that learning to ride isn't all that difficult. This coupled with the emotional high of riding often leads to overconfidence, which can lead to taking risks. Avoid this temptation! Remember, you can develop the quick subconscious responses needed to be really safe on a motorcycle only by repeatedly practicing the basic riding skills.

8. *Never use your bike as a means of taking out aggressions, showing off your skills, or expressing fearlessness.* The really smart motorcyclist is always concerned with safety—his own and others'.

9. *Be a responsible off-road rider.* Don't abuse your riding privileges. To do so may result in the closing of a designated area for off-road riding. Be courteous, respect the rights of others, and follow these guidelines:
   a. Heed all regulations.
   b. Intrude as little as possible.
   c. Avoid high speeds (unless you're in a competition or authorized motorcycle park).
   d. Make sure your machine is as quiet as possible (don't modify it to make it louder).
   e. Follow all fire safety precautions.

Suggested Reading

Cycle News, Cycle News Inc., Long Beach, CA, and Tucker, GA.

Engel, Lyle Kenyon. *The Complete Motorcycle Book*. New York: Four Winds Press, 1974.

Motorcross magazine, Daisy/Hi-Torque Publishing Company, Encino, CA.

"State Laws Related to Trail Bike Use" and *A Trail Rider's Guide to the Environment*, Department of Government Relations, American Motorcyclists Assn., Westerville, OH.

ROLLER
SKATING

Getting Started

Nowadays, it's easier than ever to get started roller skating. It seems like everybody's on wheels. Probably some of your friends are already roller skating and may even own skates. But you should start out by renting a pair to see if you like the sport, before rushing out to buy the best skates you can find.

Roller rinks, skate rental shops, and mobile skate rental trucks all rent skates by the hour, session, or day. Check around and you're likely to find a place near you that rents skates.

If you're under eighteen, most skate rental shops will require a letter from your parents or guardian granting permission for you to rent skates, or a parent or guardian must sign a release form so that the skate shop is not liable for any injuries that may occur while you're on the shop's skates. Renting skates may cost you anywhere from about $1.50–$4 an hour and $5–$11 a day, depending upon where you live. Some rental shops may also require a deposit.

To rent the best possible pair of roller skates, follow this checklist:

**The author tries her hand (foot?) at roller skating!
(Photo by Ronald Zeiger)**

1. Try to rent a pair of skates that's already broken in. They're likely to fit more comfortably.
2. Bring extra socks along so you can adjust the fit. A thin pair of cotton socks and a thick pair of wool socks is the best combination.
3. Make sure the skates you rent have been properly maintained by the rental shop.
   a. Wheels should be perfectly round and spin smoothly.
   b. There should be no play of the wheels on the axles.
   c. Toe stops should be tightly bolted on and not worn down.
   d. Trucks should be properly secured onto the plates of the skates.
   e. Laces should not be broken.
   f. Skates should be clean. Look out for muddy skates and sweaty boots—signs that the skates have not been properly maintained.

Once you've located a pair of rental skates that fit you comfortably and are in good repair, lace the boots up tightly from the toe, keeping the tongues straight. At the top of the boots the laces can be a little looser so they don't cut off circulation to your feet.

If it's your first time on skates or you haven't skated since you were a little kid, it's a good idea to rent some protective gear along with your rental skates. Knee pads, elbow pads, and wrist guards can be rented for about 50¢–$1.50 a pair for the day. Some rental shops will let you use the protective gear with no extra charge, but if they don't, it's well worth the money to rent them.

A fun way to learn how to skate is to go along with a friend who already can skate. With a friend, you can fall down together, laugh together, and most of all, have a good time. You'll also need a friend to help you stand on your skates and stay balanced, and to teach you how to go forward, backward, turn, and stop.

If you don't know anyone who can teach you, you can learn by watching other skaters and asking them questions. In addition, many roller rinks offer a series of lessons: beginner, intermediate, and advanced. Rinks that are affiliated with the Roller Skating Rink Operators' Association conduct especially good beginners' classes. Magazines such as *Roller Skating* feature helpful tips, and several good roller skating books include excellent chapters on beginning techniques (see "Suggested Reading").

No matter how you learn to skate, you're bound to fall at the beginning. So you might as well know how to fall correctly. If you feel as if you're going to fall, or that you must fall to avoid running into something, try to fall forward instead of backward. If you can, steer yourself toward a soft, grassy area and with your arms bent, try to roll as you fall. Land, if you can, on whatever protective pads you're wearing or on the padded parts of your body.

To avoid injuring muscles you may have not used for a long time, remember to warm up and warm down before and after roller skating. Do some upper and lower leg stretches and toe touches to loosen up your muscles. Listen to your body and stop skating when your muscles feel tired. Stretch out those muscles again after skating and you won't feel stiff the next time out.

Equipment

Once you get rolling on skates, you may want to buy your own skates for the following reasons:

1. Rental skates are used by thousands of pairs of different feet, while your skates conform to only your own feet.
2. Each time you rent skates the cost adds up. That money could be going toward your own pair.
3. With your own skates, you can go roller skating anytime and anywhere without the hassle of first having to rent them.

These days buying roller skates is like buying a stereo set; you can buy them already assembled or you can buy the component parts. You can get a bargain or a custom-quality pair. Skates cost anywhere from about $39–$188, but don't buy the very bottom of the line or imports. These skates are poorly constructed. Do buy the best pair you can afford and the one most suited for the type of skating you'll be doing most often. Before you buy a pair, you should know whether you'll be using your roller skates for transportation, outdoor recreation, dance skating, figure skating, indoor rink skating, speed skating, skate park skating, or roller hockey.

You can buy complete, already assembled pairs of less expensive skates at discount, department, and sporting goods stores. But good quality, custom skates should be purchased at a specialty skate shop or at a roller rink skate shop where experienced salespeople can recommend the proper boots, skate-plate assembly, and wheels for the type of skating you want to do, as well as expertly assemble the component parts for you.

When buying the parts of your skates separately, look for boots made out of leather or suede. Avoid vinyl boots—they suffocate your feet. Manufacturers such as Reidell, Openhamer, and Hyde all have a good reputation for well-crafted boots. Boots of this quality start at about $49 and go up to $83. With that much money invested in your boots, make sure you get a good fit. Your boots should fit snugly so they can stretch and conform to your feet. If they're roomy when you first buy them, they'll soon become too loose.

A skate-plate assembly consisting of a plate on top of which the boot is mounted, two trucks, and a toe stop costs anywhere from $28–$49. A die-cast or sand-cast skate-plate assembly made of aluminum alloy is most often recommended for beginning skaters.

As for wheels, here again, experienced personnel should be able to suggest the best type of wheels for the surface you'll be skating on. In general, the smoother the surface, the harder the wheels should be. Larger, softer, hot-poured polyurethane wheels are recommended for outdoor skating, while smaller, harder polyurethane wheels are used for indoor roller rink skating. Kryptonics, Ranalli, and Gyro are highly regarded manufacturers of wheels. A set of eight wheels with full-precision bearings can cost anywhere from $38–$61.

Other accessories for roller skating include toe guards, which are protective strips of leather or heavy-duty plastic attached to the front of the boots to protect the toes from wearing out, and rubber toe stops, which not only protect the toes but are used to stop when skating backward or very slowly forward.

For your own protection, when first learning to skate, you should wear a long-sleeved shirt and pants or jeans. For greater protection, wrist guards, knee and elbow pads, and gloves are also advisable. Wrist guards cost anywhere from $11–$22 and are made of suede, leather, or nylon. Buy the type with a plastic insert, which will help prevent you from breaking your wrists should you fall (broken wrists are the most common skating injury). Knee and elbow pads cost anywhere from $8–$28 a pair. Look for the type with a plastic cup; this type offers better joint protection. Leather gloves with pads in the palm are best. Gloves can cost anywhere from $8–$28. If you plan to play roller hockey or skate in a skate park, you'll also need a helmet. Make sure the helmet you buy completely covers your head, fits tightly, and has a heavy chin strap. Helmets cost $16–$33.

Getting Involved

Once you've mastered the fundamentals of roller skating—skating forward and backward, and stopping in both directions—and have gone skating several times at your local park or rink, you'll probably be ready for some new challenges. To expand your basic skills, you can learn such moves as forward and backward

crossover turns, the Three Turn, and the Spread
Eagle and Mohawks turns. Next you can progress to showy moves like Shoot the Duck,
where you skate forward in a squat position
with one leg extended straight out in front of
you; and the arabesque, where you glide forward on one skate, lift the other leg straight up
behind you, and extend your arms and hands

**These wheels experts weave their way through a
tricky course. (Jeffrey Werner)**

outward in a graceful position.

If learning fancy jumps and spins appeals to you, you can enroll in group or private lessons in figure, freestyle, or dance roller skating.

A whole new curved, sculptured, concrete world awaits the roller skater who gets involved in radical terrain skating in skate parks. Bowls, which are basins 7 to 12 feet in depth with graduated sides; full- and half-circle pipes; pools with coped edges; ramps; runs; and freestyle areas make up the landscape of a skate park. To use these facilities, you'll have to pay an admission fee and you must wear a helmet, gloves, and knee and elbow pads. If you're under eighteen your parents must sign a liability release form. Although there are areas for beginners, skate parks are for roller skaters who have *totally mastered all the beginning skills,* know how to skate forward and backward and how to stop, and are good skaters on flat terrain.

There are no radical terrain skating instructors at skate parks, so you'll have to learn the moves by trial and error and by watching others. To work up to the more vertical planes in the park, skate the gently banked walls first. With enough practice, you'll be able to do such moves as the outside or frontside turn, balancing on the coping of a pool-type bowl, and jumping up in the air to make a turn. These days, when it comes to doing stunts on wheels, the sky's the limit!

Inside Tips From the Experts

Jim Sniadach, retail manager of a skate shop, offers these tips to beginning skaters:

1. Learn to stand on one skate and find your balance. While standing on one skate, practice moving your other foot forward, backward, and all around.
2. Once you've found your balance, practice walking on your toe stops so that you can later do jump starts and stops. Learning to walk on your toe stops will help prevent you from falling so much.
3. Learn how to fall. You're going to take falls when you try new things. So prepare yourself. Go into a grassy field and practice rolling and falling on the padded areas of your body.
4. Wear protective equipment, and especially wrist guards, which protect you from breaking your wrists.
5. Don't kid yourself. The most dangerous thing about skating is the skater. Be cautious. Use good judgment. Don't attempt something difficult without instruction or supervision.
6. Keep your skates well maintained. Make sure all parts are properly secured. Give your skates a periodic safety check.

Suggested Reading

Phillips, Ann-Victoria. The Complete Book of Roller Skating. New York: Workman Publishing Company, 1979.

"Roller Skating for Exercise" and "This is Roller Skating," Roller Skating Rink Operators of America, Lincoln, NE.

Roller Skating magazine, Surfer Publishing Group, Inc., Dana Point, CA.

SKATEBOARDING

Getting Started

If you can run and have fairly good balance (or even if you don't), you're ready to start skateboarding!

To begin, borrow or buy a skateboard that doesn't have wobbly, hard wheels. Look for one with moderately soft urethane wheels and stable turning action. Choose a narrower board rather than a wider board at first (a smaller board and smaller wheels give you more control). Wear tennis shoes with a thin sole, so you can "feel" the board, and a heavy, long-sleeved shirt and thick pants to protect you should you fall. For added protection, padded gloves and elbow pads are also advisable.

To get the feel of the board, try standing on it on a carpet or lawn where the skateboard won't roll. Set your feet diagonally on the board. Tip the board from side to side to see how this movement steers it.

Now you're ready to move from your grassy or carpeted area to a slight incline. Look for a smooth, slight slope with a soft runoff, such as a concrete, pebble-free path that winds its way through lawns in a park. Put your front foot on the board first. Push off slowly and easily with your back foot, then put it on the board, and coast down the incline. Keep your knees bent and stay as loose as you can. If you think you're going to fall, fall forward and roll with your arms bent.

Turning on the skateboard is done by leaning. Don't lean with your body stiff from head to toe, as if you were a telephone pole. Move the middle of your body to one side or the other, and no matter how far you lean, hold your head straight up. Keep your knees bent during all turns.

As you move from gentle slopes to steeper grades, you'll need to learn how to traverse, or "slalom." This means going across the slope rather than straight down it, turning sharply and cutting across again and again. You may need to loosen the action of the trucks that hold the wheels and allow them to steer. Adjust the action bolts with a wrench, and make sure the locknuts are tight.

Here's one last, basic beginner's tip: how to stop! If you're going slowly enough, you can drag your pushing foot against the sidewalk until you and your board slow down to a stop. Step off the board quickly and stop the board either with your foot or simply by picking it up. Another common stop is the running step-off, where you bring your pushing foot even with the front of the board and then step off with that same foot. Your other foot steps ahead of the first foot as if you were running. Continue running for a few feet until you can slow down to a stop.

Equipment

You can buy a skateboard with the component parts—the board or top, trucks, and wheels—already assembled for you, but most teenagers prefer to buy the parts separately and get better quality put-together-yourself units. The cheapest assembled skateboards are usually made of lower-grade woods, harder wheels, and weaker, single-action trucks that are often screwed on haphazardly. If you can afford to, avoid buying these skateboards of lesser quality.

Here's what to look for when buying components:

The board or top—This should be as light and strong as possible, and long and wide enough for you to stand on comfortably. Some skateboarders prefer the very wide boards, but these often hit the wheels when turned sharply. High-quality wood and epoxy plastic go into the best boards. Expensive, space-age boards cost more, but for most beginners an adequate wood or wood-and-plastic laminated top can be purchased for $11–$39.

Trucks—The trucks are the parts that hold the wheels and allow them to steer. Look for double-action trucks made of high-grade cast aluminum with axles made of high-quality steel, as thick and strong as you can find, so the axles won't bend. Good quality trucks can cost from $11–$17 apiece.

Wheels—When it comes to wheels, try to buy the best you can afford. Not only are good ones easier to ride on, but they're also safer. You may be tempted to buy a set of very wide wheels, but resist the temptation; they have a tendency to hit the bottom of the board. Buy a standard-sized set of good quality, soft, bouncy, hot-poured urethane wheels. For this type of wheel, be prepared to pay $7–$11 per wheel.

Here are some tips for assembling your skateboard components:

1. Make sure the trucks are centered and straight on the board. Draw a line down the center of the board to help you mount them.
2. Use aircraft nylock nuts and tighten them thoroughly, so your hardware won't rattle loose.

Tom Cuthbertson, author of *Anybody's Skateboard Book*, believes that "all beginners should wear wrist guards, hip pads, elbow pads, and even a helmet. The good thing about padding is that it not only makes skating safer, it makes you *feel* safer and more confident, so you learn faster." The safety equipment worn for skateboarding is the same as the protective gear worn for roller skating (see "Equipment" in the "Roller Skating" section for details and prices).

Getting Involved

Once you've learned the basics and feel confident on a skateboard, a variety of thrills awaits you. Some spills are bound to go along with the thrills, so be certain that you've learned how to fall with a roll onto the most padded parts of your body and that you wear protective gear at all times. To further avoid hurting yourself (and others), don't skate on wet pavement or in areas where there is heavy foot or street traffic.

For new challenges, you might want to get involved in:

Downhill riding, where you slalom your way with a lot of quick turns down steep hills without picking up speed. With practice you can even learn to slide in turns to control speed.

Freestyle riding, which includes "pumping" your board around on a flat, open area with a smooth concrete or asphalt surface, as well as performing tricks such as wheelies, kick turns, endovers, handstands, jumps, and whatever else your imagination comes up with.

Radical terrain riding, which is the exotic part of skateboarding. *Wait until you've thoroughly mastered the basics* before you try this aspect of the sport. It involves skating on every kind of curved, banked, or tilted surface you can find. Skateparks have lots of challenging pools, pipes, and serpentine courses. Empty swimming pools are fun and big drainage pipes are sought out, but *don't skate where it's illegal.*

Do whatever kind of free-falling, high-curving, high-turning maneuvers seem to fit the time and place. But build up from the simpler moves to the more radical, from the less tilted terrain to the vertical.

When you've conquered all the hills, freestyle, and radical terrain in your neighborhood, think about competitions such as downhill slalom and speed races, freestyle shows and contests, and the high-rolling theater of pool competition. For listings of these events and information on how to enter them, check *Skateboarder* magazine (see "Suggested Reading").

Practicing skateboard maneuvers. (Photo by Ronald Zeiger)

Inside Tips From the Experts

Tom Cuthbertson, author of *Anybody's Skateboard Book,* suggests:

1. For a beginner, the biggest trick is keeping your weight balanced right above the middle of the board while keeping your knees bent and flexible.
2. For downhill riding, know your top speed and keep below it. Once you've gone past a speed you can control, there is not much you can do to get it down to your safe level.

3. The key to freestyle riding is practice. To keep the repetition from getting boring, do it to music. It all looks best when it's done like a dance.
4. Try radical terrain skating, but not until you're ready. Make sure you've learned the moves—and put on safety equipment—before you get up on the vertical wall.
5. No matter what kind of skating you try or where you do it, wear the necessary equipment and know how to roll when you fall, instead of bouncing, scraping, and rounding off all your sharp edges!

Suggested Reading

Cuthbertson, Tom. *Anybody's Skateboard Book.* Berkeley: Ten Speed Press, 1976.

Skateboarder magazine, Surfer Publishing Group, Inc., Dana Point, CA.

Weir, LaVada. *Skateboards and Skateboarding: The Complete Beginner's Guide.* New York: Julian Messner, 1977.

SURFING

Getting Started

Learning to balance on a moving surfboard with water rushing all around you is tricky and requires time and effort, but fortunately the younger you are when you start, the easier it is to pick up surfing skills. No matter how old you are when you begin, you'll need to be in fairly good shape and at least an average swimmer. When you're first learning how to get out to the waves, you'll be using your "paddling" muscles more than you've ever used them before, and even if you are in top condition, you're likely to feel pretty tired and "rubber-armed" after your first couple of surfing sessions. Return to shore before you become overly tired or cold. Continue learning or practicing another day. Don't overextend yourself when you're just beginning.

If you don't know an experienced surfer who can introduce you to the sport, you might want to enroll in a beginner's course. A surf shop, beach area Y, or your Parks and Recreation Department may either offer lessons, or be able to recommend someone who does. Some schools, Y's, and Explorer troops now include surfing in their programs.

If lessons aren't available where you live, you

can learn the basics of surfing — how to paddle, catch waves, turn, keep out of the way of other surfers so you don't "drop-in" on them, and other "rules of the road" — on a boogie or belly board. In a prone position with the upper part of your body against one of these small-sized boards, you get the feel of surfing without the added difficulty of having to spring up to a standing positon and balance on a board.

When you're ready for a regular-sized surfboard, here are some hints to help you get started:

1. Find out where the *safest* and best waters are for beginning surfers. Check with more experienced surfers, surf shops and schools, and surfing guidebooks to the coastal waters nearest you. You're looking for a place with a sandy beach and sandy bottom or reef, where the waves break gently and consistently a moderate distance from shore, giving you time to stand up and ride.

2. *Never surf alone. Always bring a buddy along,* preferably one who can help you with the basics.

3. Before getting out into the waves, wax the top of your surfboard from tip to tip and rail to rail. (The new, "soft" boards don't need waxing.) Use plain paraffin or surf wax appropriate to the water temperature in your area. You can buy it at surf shops.

4. To paddle out, lie flat on your board. Using the swimmer's crawl stroke, paddle out to the left or right of a pack of surfers. Remember, the fin or skeg goes down into the water and to the back of the surfboard.

5. Before tackling the wave's face, ride in on several white water waves (or soup) on your belly, then your knees, and eventually standing up.

6. To get the hang of standing quickly on your board, practice at home. Lie flat with your belly against the floor and practice springing up from this position to a standing position, using your arms as if you were doing a push-up. Land with either foot forward, whichever feels best, and your other foot in back of and perpendicular to the front foot. If you stand with your right foot forward, that's the "goofy-foot" stance. Left foot forward is the standard stance, but do what feels most comfortable.

7. When you're ready to catch your first wave, don't drop-in on the waves of more experienced surfers. Aim your board straight to shore. When you see a good wave approaching, paddle to keep ahead of it. When you feel your board lift up behind you and start to accelerate down the face of the wave, jump up as quickly as possible into the surfer's stance. Stand two-thirds of the way back on the board and try to keep the nose about 2 inches above the water.

8. Don't try turning until you've ridden the wave most of the way in. You'll have enough to concentrate on just keeping your balance.

9. If more experienced surfers are in your path, give them the right of way.

10. Groups of waves are called sets. They usually come every 10 or 15 minutes. A good

wave to catch in a set is one that peaks up higher and is thinner and steeper on the face than the other waves.

11. You can also practice your stance and balance on a skateboard. When you've got the feel of the board, practice turns and kickouts.

Equipment

Before investing in surfing equipment, rent a surfboard and wet suit to make sure you like the sport and want to get more involved in it.

To help you rent the right board, *Surfer* magazine suggests:

For the first outing or two, choosing a board involves probably renting or borrowing until you gain enough basic board savvy to be able to recognize the board you'll want to buy to continue learning on for a while. Any established, reputable surf shop (ask a few surfers to recommend a good one) generally has boards to rent. The main things to consider: (A) Use a board that's in pretty good condition with no jagged, damaged areas in the fiberglass outer shell that could cut or scratch. (B) Use a board that's long enough (at least in the 8-foot range) and wide enough (21 inches or more at the widest point) to float and plane easily. When starting off a board really can't be too big. When lying prone on the board with your weight evenly distributed just a taste back of dead center, the tail of the board should not sink below the surface more than an inch or so, with the nose (front tip) clearing the surface by a similar amount as you glide forward.[1]

Renting a board costs anywhere from about $6–$11 a day. Some shops require a deposit. If you're under eighteen, some places will require you to have an adult rent the board for you. Try to rent a "soft" board rather than a conventional one. If you have to rent a conventional one, the wider it is, the better, but not so wide that you can't carry it under one arm. Holding the board horizontally, it should fit under your armpit so that with your arm at your side, your fingers just curl around the rail (the edge of the surfboard).

In most coastal waters where the temperature of the ocean is usually below 68°, you'll need to rent a wet suit. Renting one will cost about $6–$11 a day, and a deposit may be required. Here again, if you're under eighteen an adult may have to rent it for you. Surf shops rent wet suits and will give you the one best suited for the temperature of the water in your area. Make sure it fits snugly.

Eventually, if you continue surfing, you'll want to buy your own equipment. You might consider buying a used board at first because it will get "dinged" while you're still learning. If you're lucky, for about $55 you can pick up an old-style long board at a garage sale or flea market, or from another surfer. These boards are 8 feet long and 22 inches wide; they make ex-

---

[1]"Getting Started — Safer, Quicker, Easier," *Surfer*, July, 1979, p. 23.

cellent boards for beginners.

If you can't come across a used long board, your next best bet is to purchase a new soft board, which is less expensive than other new ones. These polyethylene boards cost $188–$199. Soft boards are good beginning boards because they float well, enable you to catch and ride smaller waves, and won't get dinged. In addition, if your soft board accidentally hits you, you won't get hurt.

When your skills warrant a fiberglass, shorter board you can expect to pay anywhere from $264–$330.

When buying a wet suit, an experienced salesperson in a surf shop should help you select the appropriate one for the water temperature in your coastal area. Wet suits come in different thicknesses, or weights, of neoprene. They also come in several styles: full suit with long sleeves and long legs, spring suit with short sleeves and short legs, sleeveless short johns and long johns, and a two-piece outfit consisting of a jacket and long johns. Depending on the weight and style you choose, wet suits can cost anywhere from $99–$275.

Avoid buying the cheapest suit possible. A good quality wet suit often comes with a guarantee, wears better, and can usually be resold for close to the the original price. Look for nylon taped seams and plastic zippers in the better wet suits. Buy a suit a little big, to allow for growth, but not too big or it won't keep you warm and the water will flow through it. Make sure a qualified salesperson checks the fit of your suit.

Besides surf wax, another accessory you'll have to purchase is a surf leash. *Surfer* magazine offers this advice about this important accessory:

> For the protection of others as well as yourself, wear a surf leash. This is an elastic cord attached to the rear of the board at one end and to your ankle with a quick release Velcro strap at the other end. An experienced surfer or shop salesman will help you select a good leash.[2]

Getting Involved

Once you can successfully catch waves and feel comfortable on your surfboard, you'll need to learn how to turn your board to increase the length of your ride on the wave's face. You'll want to master such turns as the rear-foot turn, where the position of the rear foot is moved to make the board turn either left or right; the leaning turn, where the feet are stationary, but the weight of the surfer's heels is shifted to cause the board to turn; and the kick turn, where the surfer steps quickly to the back of the board with the rear foot and twists the body to jerk the board nose into a new position. Once you've learned the kick turn, you can use this maneuver to do a kickout to end your ride on a wave in style.

As soon as you can make these turns automatically, you're ready for walking on your

---

[2]"Getting Started — Safer, Quicker, Easier," *Surfer*, July, 1979, p. 23.

"Hanging five," or riding in a forward trim with one foot over the nose of the board. (Courtesy of *Surfer* magazine)

board and other surfing tricks. Using either of two walking techniques — the shuffle step and the cross-over step — you can move up to the nose of your board and "hang-five" or "hang-ten" (toes) over the edge while skimming the surf. For a really thrilling ride, you can learn to do the Roller Coaster, where you turn your board sharply and hit the top of the wave, then turn the board toward shore and back into the wave again.

Now that you're beyond the beginner's stage, you'll probably want to go to a shorter board for more maneuverability. With a short board, you can get into the more critical part of the wave and execute a trick known as Getting Tubed. If you catch the right wave, you can actually ride inside its hollow part or tube — a thrill that lasts only a few seconds, but surfers consider it the ultimate in surfing tricks.

Inside Tips From the Experts

Jim Gordan, experienced surfer and salesman of surfing equipment, offers these tips to beginning surfers:

1. *Don't surf alone or in hazardous waters.*
2. If the water temperature warrants it, keep yourself warm by wearing a wet suit that fits snugly but comfortably. Loss of body heat brings about a loss of energy, increasing your chances of drowning.
3. Watch and learn from experienced surfers.
4. Be respectful of better surfers, and try to get along with all your fellow surfers.
5. Lots of practice makes a good surfer.

Suggested Reading

Dixon, Peter. *The Complete Book of Surfing.* New York: Coward-McCann, Inc., 1965

Olney, Ross. *The Young Sportsman's Guide to Surfing.* New York: Scholastic Book Services, 1968.

Surfer magazine, Surfer Publications, Inc., Dana Point, CA.

UNICYCLING

Getting Started

Getting started on a one-wheeled cycle is just about as easy as learning to ride a two-wheeler for the first time. Here's how you do it!

Find a smooth, level, concrete or blacktop open area; for instance, a schoolyard or a long driveway next to a wall.

Make sure that your unicycle seat is adjusted to your size. The saddle should be adjusted so that when you sit on it with the ball of your foot on the pedal in its lowest position, your leg is almost straight. If you have to change the seat height, don't forget to tighten all the bolts, especially the saddle clamps.

Next, place the rear of the wheel against a block of wood to prevent the unicycle from moving backward. Position the wheel firmly against the block with the pedals parallel to the ground. The left pedal should be forward and the right pedal back. Now you're ready to get on. Get a friend to help you.

To mount, stand behind your unicycle, holding the front of the seat in your right hand. Support yourself by holding on to your friend's hand with your left hand, held slightly above waist height. Step onto the right pedal by placing your right instep on the outside edge of the pedal, and position the seat under you. If you apply pressure to the right pedal, the wheel will hold its position against the block. Now push down on the left pedal and start to move forward, holding on to your support with your left hand. Keep your back straight, hold your head and shoulders up, lean slightly forward, and focus your eyes straight ahead of you. Make sure to keep all your weight on the seat, not on the pedals.[3]

As your ability increases, try riding with the aid of a wall beside you instead of your assistant. Find a stretch of sidewalk with a wall beside it, high enough to touch when you ride along side. Find something to hold on to as you mount your unicycle. Then lean on the wall and ride parallel to it, moving your hand along the wall to maintain your balance. Practice this routine in both directions, until you feel ready to push off and ride free of the wall.

Once you can ride without any support, use your arms to help maintain your balance. Hold your arms out straight from your body and above your waist. If you begin to lean toward one side, bring the arm on that side toward your body to help regain your balance. Once you've regained it, move your arm out again. If you feel as if you're losing your forward balance, speed up the pedal action. If you sense that you're losing your backward balance, slow down the pedal action. When riding a unicycle seems to you as easy as riding a bicycle, you're ready to try some turns and stunts.

---

[3]*Schwinn Owner's Manual: Unicycle*, Schwinn Bicycle Company, 1977, pp. 6–7.

Equipment

Most manufactured unicycles are available in two sizes, a 20″ and a 24″ wheel. The 20″ wheel unicycle is easier to maneuver and is recommended for beginners of all ages. It is also the unicycle to use if you're interested in stunt riding. A unicycle with a 24″ wheel is recom-

Riding the forty-two and forty-three inch big wheel unicycles. (Courtesy of William Jenack)

mended for moderate distance riding as the larger wheel allows you to go farther and faster with less effort than the smaller.[4]

To find the correct size, determine your leg length by measuring the distance from your crotch to the floor (wear flat-heeled shoes). Check the following chart* for your frame size and saddle post requirement:

Frame Size	Wheel Size	Saddle Post Size	Leg Length to Floor
20″	20″	Standard-9″	27″ to 31″
20″	20″	Special-14″	32″ to 36″
24″	24″	Standard-9″	29″ to 33″
24″	24″	Special-14″	34″ to 38″

Choose a unicycle and saddle post combination in which the saddle height falls about midway between the minimum and maximum saddle heights. If you're still growing, choose a frame and saddle post combination where your leg length is closer to the minimum.

Unicycles made of high-carbon steel with vinyl saddles are available at most bicycle shops. The 20″ and 24″ unicycles cost around $94. The 6′ giraffe model runs around $165.

When riding a unicycle, wear trouser clips at the bottom of long pants as you would when riding a bicycle. To protect your ankles from rubbing against the crank, wear ankle-high

[4]*Schwinn Owner's Manual: Unicycle,* Schwinn Bicycle Company, 1977, p 3.

* Schwinn Unicycle Frame Sizes Chart reprinted with the permission of the Schwinn Bicycle Company.

shoes or boots with a good-size heel that can hook behind the pedal. Other than these protective requirements, you can ride a unicycle in any comfortable clothes.

Getting Involved

Once you can ride forward in a straight line, you can learn to make quarter-turns, half-turns, complete circles, and patterns such as the figure-8 and the snake. Making a turn is fairly easy; after a short time riding you may find yourself making them automatically. To turn, you simply rotate the arms and upper body in the opposite direction of the desired turn.

Once you've mastered turns, you're ready to learn how to rock and how to ride backwards. To rock your unicycle, ride forward, pause, half-pedal backwards, then ride forward again. Practice rocking until you can do it with either pedal forward. When you can successfully do one rocking motion, practice doing two in a row, then three, and so on. To ride backwards, start by riding forward, pausing, then pedaling backwards. Have an assistant hold one hand when you're just learning how to ride backwards. When you can ride backwards for 25 feet or more without someone holding your hand, then you can try making turns, circles, and patterns while pedaling backwards.

Eventually you can combine unicycling with other skills — Frisbee disc throwing, juggling, and yo-yo playing (see individual chapters on these skills). You can also do stunts with a partner or learn to ride either a midget unicycle or a 6-footer (known as a giraffe). All these skills and more are fully described in the only book written on the subject, Jack Wiley's *The Unicycle Book* (see "Suggested Reading").

If you become interested enough in unicycling, find out if there's a unicycle club in your area. If there isn't, you can teach your friends how to ride and form your own club. As a member of a club, you can organize group rides, work up your own routines, or ride in parades. Many clubs sponsor unicycle competitions. These contests have included such events as sprint and distance racing, and individual and team trick riding. Your club can hold its own day of contests, including relay races, backward racing, slalom racing, hill climbing, and one-leg races, or any combination of events you choose to organize. Information on how to run unicycling competitions is included in *The Unicycle Book*.

Inside Tips From the Experts

The following riding tips for unicyclists appear on pp. 11–12 of the *Schwinn Owner's Manual: Unicycle*.

1. *Obey this simple rule for safety when unicycling.* When learning to control and ride the unicycle, be cautious where you practice and ride. Always practice and ride in an open area away from people and property.
2. *Keep all your weight on the saddle.* The theory that applies when riding a unicycle is to keep the center of gravity over the axle. This is accomplished by keeping your weight

on the saddle, not on the pedals.

3. *Keep your back straight.* It is very important that you keep your back straight because this helps in keeping your weight over the wheel axle.

4. *Keep your head up and eyes forward.* It is helpful in maintaining your balance to keep your head up with eyes forward. Don't look down.

5. *Lean slightly in the direction you are pedaling.* When you pedal forward, lean slightly forward to bring your body weight forward of the axle.

Suggested Reading

Schwinn Owner's Manual: Unicycle. Chicago: Schwinn Bicycle Company, 1977.

Wiley, Jack. *The Unicycle Book.* Harrisburg, PA: Stackpole Books, 1974.

YO-YO PLAYING

Getting Started

To get properly started in yo-yo play, it's extremely important to use a spinning or trick yo-yo, one that "sleeps" (spins or sticks) at the end of the string. Avoid a beginner's yo-yo that can't sleep and can only go up and down, as it is not possible to do any yo-yo tricks with it. The yo-yo to use is one with a double-twisted string that is looped around the axle, not knotted to it.

Once you have the proper yo-yo — one with a loop at the end of the string — here's how to get it ready for play:

1. Let the yo-yo string out to its full length. Holding the yo-yo between your two feet, measure your string to four inches above your waist. Cut off any excess.
2. Make a new loop at the top of the string. Then pull part of the string through the loop to form a slip-loop.
3. Place the slip-loop around your middle finger just behind your first knuckle with the knot on the inside of your finger..
4. If you're using a new yo-yo or string, before winding the string, spin your yo-yo a few times to the right to tighten it. To loosen the string if it becomes too tight, spin the yo-yo

to the left. Remember: *right is tight; left is loose.*

5. To wind up your yo-yo, hold the string about two inches from the yo-yo. Wind it loosely and slowly around the axle in a clockwise direction until you can wind it tightly. Then wind up the rest of the way.

Now you're ready to learn the simplest, but most important, yo-yo trick — the spinner. This basic trick is the beginning of many more difficult tricks. To do it, hold the yo-yo in the palm of your hand with your palm up. Make sure the string leads off from the top of the yo-yo. Bend your arm at the elbow. Snap your wrist downward throwing the yo-yo out in an arc in front of you. When it completely unwinds, stop your hand and allow it to sleep, or spin, at the end of the string for a few seconds. Be careful not to let the spinning yo-yo hit the ground. After it has spun for a few seconds, turn your hand over so that your palm is down. Give the yo-yo a slight jerk and it will return to your hand. Be sure to catch the returning yo-yo with your palm down. Practice making your yo-yo sleep for a longer and longer time. The harder you throw it down, the longer it will sleep. The longer it stays down, the easier it will be for you to execute a trick. According to yo-yo professional Bob Rule, you need to sleep the yo-yo only 6 to 8 seconds to perform the most difficult of tricks.

Equipment

A number of trick or spinning yo-yos work

well for the novice: the Duncan Imperial, molded from high-quality plastic in assorted colors; the Duncan Butterfly, with the yo-yo halves reversed, making it easier to do string tricks; and the Duncan Wheels, a Butterfly yo-yo with a chrome-mag insert. (Duncan is the registered trademark of the Flambeau Products Corporation.) These yo-yos cost from about $2–$3.50.

Two models of Pro-Yos are the Wheeler and the Deluxe. (Pro-Yo is the registered trademark of Duracraft, Inc.) They are also excellent choices for those just starting out in yo-yo play. Pro-Yos feature a flywheel design that distributes 80% of the weight to the rim for 30% to 40% longer spin. To further increase length of spin, the axle diameter of these yo-yos has been reduced from the standard .250″ to .150″. The longer spinning features make it easier for beginners to learn to do tricks and enable advanced players to glide through different tricks with greater control and ease. Additional features of the Pro-Yo include a beveled hex-axle that self-centers the string and pop-out side discs that enable you to pop in your favorite pictures and emblems. These Pro-Yos cost about $1.50–$2.50.

Advanced players will also enjoy playing with either the Duncan Professional, with its axle designed for less string wear and quicker reaction to tricks, or the flywheel design Ultimate Pro-Yo, featuring a wooden axle for longer spin, greater control, and reliability. These yo-yos cost about $3.50–$5.50.

For yo-yos with novelty as well as spin, there's the "Be-A-Sport" line of Festival yo-yos shaped like baseballs, basketballs, golf balls, bowling balls, and hockey pucks. Another sporty yo-yo is made by Duracraft and features the logos of the twenty-eight teams in the National Football League on the sides of the Pro-Yo Wheeler. All these yo-yos cost about $2.

The No-Jive three-in-one yo-yo by Tom Kuhn Custom Yo-Yos is a handsome, wooden model that can be unscrewed for easy knot removal and put together again in three different positions. It also features interchangeable parts and is sold with spare wooden axles, screws, hexnuts, and a spool of string. Two laser-carved models by Tom Kuhn Custom Yo-Yos are the Flying Camel and the Mandala. For these precision-crafted, smooth-playing, long-spinning, all-wooden yo-yos, be prepared to pay about $14.50–$22.

A neat beginner's yo-yo guide is Helane Zeiger's *World on a String*, which contains easy-to-follow instructions accompanied by clear illustrations and photographs of 70 yo-yo tricks: 10 basic tricks, 27 intermediate tricks, and 33 advanced tricks.

Getting Involved

Once you can successfully do the Spinner, you can learn other basic tricks such as Walk-the-Dog, Johnny-Round-the-Corner (also known as Orbit Launch), and Rock-the-Baby. When you've mastered these tricks you can advance to such tricks as Man-on-the-Flying-Trapeze, Skyrocket, and the Creeper (also known as Landrover), and later to such advanced tricks as One-Handed Star, Eiffel Tower, and the Motorcycle.

When you can do all of the one-handed tricks fully described in *World on a String* or the *Duncan Yo-Yo Trick Book* (see "Suggested Reading"), then you're ready to try two-handed tricks. You can learn these tricks from the books mentioned, from other yo-yo players, or from

A perfect Rock-the-Baby. (UPI)

yo-yo professionals who make appearances in different regions of the country from time to time.

Inside Tips From the Experts

Helane Zeiger, yo-yo professional and author of World On A String, offers these tips to beginning yo-yo players:

1. If your string develops a knot, gets tangled in the yo-yo, or becomes frayed or worn, you can buy a new yo-yo string without buying a new yo-yo. (Sold in packages where yo-yos are sold.)
2. Remove old string by untwisting the double string at the base of the yo-yo, and slipping the loop off the axle and over one of the yo-yo halves.
3. Remove any fragments of old string before putting on the new one. Be careful not to scratch the yo-yo axle with whatever tool you use.
4. Untwist the bottom of your new string and slip it over one of the yo-yo halves and onto the axle. Tighten by spinning it a few times to the right as you would for a new yo-yo. Don't forget to measure the string to your size and to make a new slip-loop if necessary.
5. Do not attempt to repair a broken string by knotting it. The knot will slow down the action of the yo-yo and get caught in it.
6. Play with your yo-yo in open spaces clear of people and breakable objects. Check to make sure no one is in front or back of you before doing tricks such as Around-the-World.

Suggested Reading

Duncan Yo-Yo Trick Book. Baraboo, WI: Flambeau Products Corp., 1979.

Malko, George. *The One and Only Yo-Yo Book.* New York: Avon Books, 1978.

Zeiger, Helane. *World on a String: The How-To Yo-Yo Book.* Chicago: Contemporary Books, 1979.